THE 6 SYMBOLS OF THE GOSPEL

THE WHOLE STORY OF GOD'S REDEMPTIVE LOVE

Dr. Mark McNees
with Dr. John Bickley

Triumph Media

Mark's Dedication

I would like to dedicate this book to the people who make up Element3 Church, it has been through my many conversations with you over the years that I have forged and refined the ideas presented in this book.

John's Dedication

To my beautiful, selfless, and encouraging wife and to the greatest gift God ever granted both of us, our bright-eyed daughter.

CONTENTS

Appendices

Acknowledgments

Writing my second book has been one of the hardest things I have ever done in my life, and there is no way it could have been completed without the help, input, and long-suffering of many people. I would like to thank:

John Bickley for meeting with me every Friday over coffee for months to hash out all these ideas and help organize them into a coherent book. It would not have happened without you.

My wife **Shannon** and kids (**Madison** and **Eric**) who encouraged me along the way.

Mona Lewis for being the first brave soul to read and edit this book.

Amy Gwartney for the final edits and encouragement.

Eric Case for reading it before it was edited and offering some great insight on the Holy Spirit.

Dan Meyer for also reading it before it was edited and offering some wonderful suggestions on how to refine and make this book more accessible.

Sam Nunnally for the verbal processing, encouragement, and pushing this project through to the endzone.

Katie Reeves (www.ktcreative.net) for putting her professional touches on the cover and formatting the book.

Donna Irene Muccio (www.donnairenephotography.com) for taking such wonderful pictures of John and me.

Rebekah Hagen, Judy Abbott, Rebecca White, Amanda Matthews, and Theresa Bogema for reading my blog and helping me refine many of these ideas.

Element3 Church for being so supportive and blessing me with so many experiences.

Thomasville Growth Group for pre-reading and being a test group for the group studies.

Michael Hanna for reading a greatly marked up copy and taking this project so seriously.

Martha Hanna for doing an amazing job proofing the book.

Lori Abbey for taking the time to proof the book.

Dr. Tim Singletary for believing in me and this project.

Mark Duvall for your constant friendship, counsel, and music through the years.

The ideas in this book are from years of sitting under great teaching and reading amazing books. I tried to credit everyone for their contribution to this book but I am sure I missed someone. I would like to make special note of Leonard Sweet, Scot McKnight, N.T. Wright, Seth Godin, Erwin McManus, Malcolm Gladwell, Chip and Dan Heath, and Dietrich Bonhoeffer. Your books and teachings have impacted me and formed my thinking. The words in this book are echoes of your brilliant thoughts, and I only can pray that this small work brings honor to you.

Foreword

Our God is the God of the beginning and the end, the whole story, start to finish. He enters into our individual lives, meets us where we are, with all our miscellaneous quirks and personal limits, then pulls us out of ourselves and shows us our place in his great story of relational reconciliation.

God's good news, the Gospel, is about inclusion, connection, restoration. As such, the Gospel is the antidote to our culture's current trend toward a fragmented understanding of our place in the world and history. The Gospel tells us we don't have to remain on our islands (or remain kicked off the island, depending on your perspective). The Gospel is about weaving the lives of individuals into the life of Christ and the lives of others, and revealing how this beautiful entanglement of lives works together in the full arc of God's transcendent narrative.

Too often our culture hears truncated versions of the Gospel, or even man-made substitutes. But the Gospel is more than the teachings of Jesus, or even Jesus on the Cross, or even Christ resurrected. No doubt, these are crucial elements of the story of God's restorative love, and that larger truth of course can be seen in these elements. But the Bible and the history of the Church is more than the New Testament, as pivotal as it is to our understanding of God's redemptive plan. The full Gospel begins in Eden and ends in eternal relationship, and each major piece along the way depends upon the others for a complete understanding.

Mark and I hope this book will help make connections among the major phases, or acts, if you will, of God's beautiful story of His love for His creation.

John Bickley

INTRODUCTION

Ours is a visually sophisticated culture, a world of optically stunning photographs, videos, CGI, and digital billboards. It's the age of iPads, IMAXes and HD TV. It feels like every day we speak more and more in images as our technology improves exponentially.

Contrary to popular belief, this is not a new phenomenon. People have always heavily relied on images to reach others. This is especially true of symbolic images.

We have been using symbols to represent aspects of our faith from the earliest stages of Christianity. These symbols spoke to believers in a simple, direct way. After all, most believers of the early Church were unable to read or write, the printing press was centuries away, and for the first few hundred years overt communication of one's faith could be dangerous. The solution was the heavy use of symbolic communication: the Cross, the Ichthys (Fish), the Anchor, the Iota Chi (IX), the Dove, the Shepherd, the Chi Rho (XP)...

Some of these symbols have maintained cultural relevance for centuries, while others have died off, but all had a similar purpose. These symbols helped tell the story of God's love for His creation. They served to unify and encourage believers who—in the early stages of Christianity especially—felt the pressures of persecution, division, and doubt.

This book revolves around six symbols, five of which are readily recognizable to the modern Christian: the Star of David, the Chi Rho, the Cross, the Empty Tomb, and the Fish. The final symbol, Infinite Love, is a recent addition to iconography which combines one of the oldest symbols in existence, Infinity, with the pop culture symbol for Love.

Of course, as is true for all symbols, it is not the image itself, but the idea it represents that is important. Ultimately, this is not a book about symbols, but about God's love for His creation.

Each of the six symbols discussed here represents crucial aspects of the full Gospel as revealed in the Old and New Testaments. These symbols serve as a sort of visual shorthand for a story that is anything but short. A story that, in fact, spans all of history—and ultimately transcends it.

This book has been a transformative undertaking for John and me. We have had the privilege to convey many of the ideas presented in this book in various formats and forums to our gracious church, Element3 (Tallahassee, Florida).

Through these discussions we have become increasingly convinced of how crucial this subject is for the health of the modern church. It has been a wake-up call to both of us to see how ill-equipped we are as a body of believers (across denominational and nondenominational lines) to present the whole, complete Gospel in an accurate, concise, and compelling way.

In the end, we hope that these symbols will do what symbols of the faith have always done: encourage and unify as they help to tell the whole story of God's miraculous overture to man.

WHAT IS THE GOSPEL?

Like most of my writing and sermon prep, this book was inspired by conversations with people in my community, on Facebook, Twitter, or at RedEye Coffee. I often find myself engaged in discussions about the "Gospel." And more often than not, it seems these talks end up revealing a heartbreaking error and/or omission in a person's conception of what exactly constitutes the story of God, and by doing so, misses the point of the greatest story ever told.

Here are three common misconceptions I often encounter:

New Testament Christianity

New Testament Christianity, as its name indicates, ignores the Old Testament as relevant to a Christian's life. By this omission a New Testament Christian ends up with only about twenty percent of God's Word, instruction, and story of His love. I have had several conversations with New Testament Christians, all claiming the same mantra: The Old Testament is obsolete and unnecessary to Christianity. All a Christian needs to grow into full spiritual maturity is the New Testament—that's where the true Gospel is found.

Perhaps you are not so overt about your view of the Old Testament, but possibly it seems foreign and irrelevant to you, so you don't spend much time in it. I hope this discussion will help demonstrate the error of this understanding of the Gospel. Without the Old Testament, the full story of God—and our role in that story—is incomplete and ultimately incoherent.

Four Spiritual Laws Christianity

The other day I was talking with a woman who was delighted by a sermon she had heard that week she described it as "a clear presentation of the Gospel." She went on to tell me how impressed she was with the pastor who told it to her and "If only everyone could present 'the Gospel' so clearly, then everyone would know they are sinners." When I asked her to share with me the Gospel presentation she heard, she relayed a systematic and clear presentation of the Four Spiritual Laws, or the Roman Road, including the salvation bridge illustration.

In the pages to follow, I hope to give you a more complete view of the Gospel and the biblical basis of why the Four Spiritual Laws and the Romans Road are important concepts to understand the need of the Gospel, but in themselves are not the whole Gospel. Subsequently, in the final chapter, I will present an alternative illustration to use in sharing the Gospel that hopefully avoids some of the theological pitfalls inherent in the bridge illustration.

Red Letter Christianity

I think his phrase was "I just read the red." This man's approach represented that of so many others: they just read the words of Christ and skip the rest. This is even more Gospel-deficient than New Testament Christian; at least a New Testament Christian preaches the life, death, resurrection, the church, and second coming of Jesus.

The Red Letter movement in its current manifestation was made popular by the liberal theologian Jim Wallis, but the movement finds its roots with Thomas Jefferson. Leonard Sweet summarizes the creation of the red-letter Bible in the following way, "The first 'red-letter' edition of the Bible was done by Thomas Jefferson, who scissored and pasted the parts he liked into a blank notebook he entitled "The Life and Morals of Jesus of Nazareth." The parts he liked were the teachings of Jesus. The parts he didn't like were the miracles of Jesus, or what conflicted with the confines of his interpretation of conventional science.

In other words, "The Jefferson Bible," now in a Washington, D.C. museum, likes what Jesus said, but not what Jesus did. "The Jefferson Bible" closes with Matthew 27:60: "He rolled a big stone in front of the entrance to the tomb and went away." For Jefferson, the story ended with a sepulcher and a stone.

Selective Truth

These three truncated versions of Christianity illustrate a disturbing trend of selective truth rampant in 21st century Christianity. They each hold onto "truth," but not the full-story, 360-degree truth. "Truth" that only focuses on a fragment of the story merely considers it from a narrow angle and is ultimately deficient, allowing for misunderstanding and distortion.

To illustrate, let me share a selective truth story about my race in the Escape from Alcatraz Triathlon.

On the second stage of the race, the 18-mile bike portion, I was cycling up the last steep climb before the final stage, the 8-mile run. While I was climbing, a professional triathlete (who eventually went on to take second place overall in the race) passed me.

I said to myself, "I can beat this guy up the hill." I turned myself inside out to get to the summit before him. I geared up, grit my teeth and gave it all I had.

With sweat pouring down my face and my heart pounding like a 5-year-old playing bongo drums, I slowly pulled myself up alongside him. After a few seconds of locking our horns, I am proud to say, I passed him. He didn't give up so easily; we went back and forth a few more times, but as the summit approached, I gave one last push and crested the hill on my bike before him, relishing my personal victory.

Full Disclosure:
This is a completely true story; however, it is not actually what happened. How can that be? Though it's a completely true story, it is not a complete true story.

Here's the full account:
…but as the summit approached, I gave one last push and

crested the hill on my bike before him. Looking back as I began to roll down the hill, I saw him run over the summit and begin his final sprint toward the finish line.It is true that I climbed the hill before the professional triathlete, but it is also true that I was on a bike and he was running.

The Gospel is more than the New Testament, the Four Spiritual Laws, or the teachings of Jesus. The Gospel, the "Good News," is the proclamation of the whole story of God and His creation.

While my "true" Alcatraz Triathlon story might have been told with the intent to mislead the hearer, I do not believe that's the intent of most partial-Gospelers. However, the opportunities for misunderstanding with these incomplete presentations of the Gospel remain. The point is, we must guard against partial Gospels; we should tell the whole story.

THE WHOLE STORY

So what is the whole Gospel?

Gospel means Good News, and the Good News begins with the Story of Israel as recorded in the Old Testament. It is through the Old Testament narratives, prophecy, and poetry that we learn of God's unfailing love for His creation. The Gospel is a tribute to our Heavenly Father's dedication and commitment to His children, as He guides humanity from its infancy toward the emotional and spiritual comprehension of its need for His gift of a new covenant of grace.

The **Story of Israel** illuminates the Life of Christ. Without the context of the Old Testament, Christ's actions and teachings are largely incomprehensible.

The **Life of Christ** in turn shows us how to be *in* the world but not *of* the world, and provides context for the **Cross**, the turning point of history, where God, through incomprehensible sacrifice creates a way for relational reconciliation with each of us.

The **Resurrection** legitimizes the cross, presenting a radical revision of the world's conception of the path to acceptance by God, and leads to the commissioning of the **Church**.

The second coming of Christ is the culmination of the Church's ministry on earth and completes the Story of Israel by restoring God's creation to an unfettered experience of God's **Infinite Love**.

NAVIGATING THIS BOOK

We hope this book will serve as a starting place for conversations and further explorations unlocking the timeless story of God's love. This book is not intended to be a comprehensive examination of the entire story of God. Rather an overview giving a foundational understanding of how the Bible conveys God's Good News for His creation from Genesis to Revelation and a better and more complete way to present the Gospel.

This book is arranged in six sections, each focusing on a different element in the whole Gospel. We have formatted the book in such a way as to work in a group study/discussion format, with brief chapters that might serve as topics for individual meetings, and "Going Deeper" sections at the end that provide discussion/exploration questions. Whether you use this book individually or in a group setting, we hope that it will help lead you to a fuller understanding of the Good News of God, a story that ties together and transcends history—and a story into which we all have been invited to participate.

SYMBOL ONE:
THE STAR OF DAVID

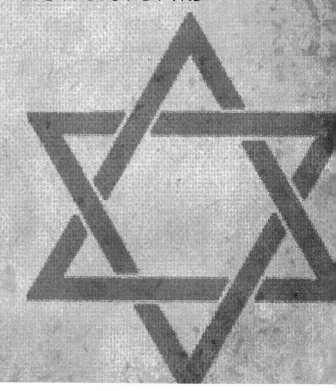

THE STORY OF ISRAEL

Depending on the biblical scholar you are reading, they will say the New Testament writers quote the Old Testament 263 to 695 times. Regardless of the biblical scholar you trust, it is obvious that the New Testament writers held the Old Testament in high regard. Not only did they quote the Old Testament, they also referenced many Old Testament men and women as examples of faith. One such example is found in Hebrews 11:39-40, "All these people earned a good reputation because of their faith, yet none of them received all that God had promised. For God had something better in mind for us, so that they would not reach perfection without us." As you will discover in this chapter, the Old Testament, The Story of Israel, is not irrelevant to the New Testament believer; in fact, it is essential to their faith.

Symbol Description: Star of David

The Star of David is an ancient symbol that has long been associated with Israel. It is a hexagram, formed by superimposing two inverted triangles (the possible meaning of which I'll discuss later). It features twelve intersection points/angles (six external, six internal), which are often associated with the twelve tribes of Israel; the Star of David is visual short-hand for Jewish history and culture.

Promises

Promises are sacred. Nothing inflicts more damage to a relationship than a broken promise, whether real or perceived.

My daughter, Madison, has a heightened sense of promise. She holds a promise—explicit and implicit alike—as a contractual obligation unbreakable by any circumstance; not even death will get you out of it.

Several years ago, it all came to a head when her mother and I informed Madison that something we had promised was not going to happen in the timeline she expected. We expressed our regret but told her it was outside of our control and we'd need to do it another time. Predictably, she had a meltdown of biblical proportions. I'm quite convinced that if God would have sent the yet unborn spirit of a scorned Madison to Egypt, Pharaoh would have not only released the Israelites immediately, but given them a ride to the Promise Land.

After enduring enough of her wrath, in frustration (when I always do my best parenting), I finally placed my hands on her shoulders, looked her in the eyes, and told her, "Listen. I PROMISE I will never make you another promise again for the rest of your life. This is an unalterable promise that will stand for all of eternity. From this point forward everything I say is subject to change as conditions warrant. This, my daughter, I PROMISE!"

OK, I know I might not make the speakers list for parenting conferences anytime soon, but the point remains: Promises matter to us, no matter the age or stage of life.

The Old Testament is in many ways a collection of promises - some of them fulfilled in the telling while others are left for future fruition. Above all else, the books of the OT establish the promise of God's grace and our redemption in the coming Messiah who will bring a restored relationship with the Father.

"Gospel" Confusion

Earlier this year, our church embarked on a journey toward Good Friday and the cross. We looked at the Old Testament's unresolved promises that were given to our ancestors in faith and we tried to experience both the anticipation and tension they must have felt by not receiving all that God had promised.

During my preparatory studies, I was struck by four things which I never fully appreciated before: the multilevel connections among the unresolved promises to the patriarchs, the resolution in Jesus, the commissioning of the church, and the second coming of Jesus.

My Mum, like Jesus' mother, is Jewish. When she was a girl, her mother gave her a gold necklace with a Star of David, much like a Christian mother would give her daughter a cross pendant. When my Mum became a follower of Christ, my Dad had a cross attached atop the Star of David. This dual-symbol charm has been a point of confusion for many of my Mum's Christian acquaintances throughout her life. They don't quite understand why she would hold on to the religion of her youth...

The tension my Mum's acquaintances experience is not uncommon for 20th and 21st century American Evangelicals. It is something, I believe, that may be traced back to a terminological mix-up, the confusion between two essential words: gospel and salvation.

The word "gospel" is the English translation of the Greek word evangel, where we get the words evangelical and evangelism. The Greek word soteria is where we derive our word "salvation."

....we have created a "salvation culture" and mistakenly understood it as a "gospel culture."

The distinction between the two, and subsequent (mis)labeling, may have led to some of the confusion many Evangelicals have with the necessity of the Story of Israel as part of the Gospel (much like New Testament Christians).

You see, many Evangelicals have mistakenly equated the word gospel with the word salvation. Theologian Scott McKnight points out the confusion of the terms:

"[Many Evangelicals] are really 'salvationists.' [...] What has happened is that we have created a 'salvation culture' and mistakenly understood it as a 'gospel culture.'"[1]

This is not to say salvation is unimportant. Salvation is clearly central to the story of God and us. It is just not the whole biblical Gospel.

The dominance of a Soterian, or salvationist, paradigm in the Western Church is fairly recent. Since the work of salvation is accomplished in the New Testament, it is the root cause of many Evangelicals' questions about what the Old Testament

---

[1] Scot McKnight, *The King Jesus Gospel: The Original Good News Revisited* (Grand Rapids, MI: Zondervan, 2011)

has to do with the Christian faith.

My Mum's conflicts over the Star of David were not confined to friends and acquaintances. Many years ago a well-known pastor was quite condescending to my Mum about her pendant, reprimanding her and insisting that she needed to be "only a Christian."

Her reply contained a profound insight. It went something like this: "I may be young and not know the New Testament as well as you, but I do know our New Testament Jesus is the foretold Messiah of the Old Testament."

Of course she is right: the story of Jesus Christ is the story of Jesus as the Jewish (and Gentile) Messiah. The word "Christ" is the Greek translation of the Hebrew word "Messiah." Both terms translate to Savior, King, and Lord. In other words "Christian" really means "follower of the Messiah"—the one promised in the OT texts.

Mary's Faith

An example of how important it is for a Christian to know the Story of Israel is found in the account of Mary's first encounter with the angel, sent from God to give her the news about her pregnancy:

"Don't be afraid, Mary," the angel told her, "for you have found favor with God! You will conceive and give birth to a son, and you will name him Jesus. He will be very great and will be called the Son of the Most High. The Lord God will give him the throne of his ancestor David. And he will reign over Israel forever; his

Kingdom will never end!" (Luke 1:30-33).

The angel just told an unmarried, teenage girl in the first century—who could, by the Law, be put to death as a result of the news—that she was pregnant...(!) Her response is remarkable: "Let what you said come to pass." (v.38)

She would not have responded with such faith, courage, and conviction unless she knew the prophecies pronounced in the Story of Israel.

This is an example of why it is so important to understand the whole Story of God, which includes the Story of Israel. That story is the basis for everything Jesus did in His life. In order to really know Jesus and be able to respond to Him in faith, like Mary responded in faith, we must know the whole story—the whole Gospel.

The authors of the New Testament make this clear. There are countless (well more than I care to count) references to the Old Testament in the New Testament. This is because Matthew, Mark, Luke, John, James, Peter, Paul, the writer of Hebrews, and Jesus all knew that the story of Israel was essential context for understanding and responding to the life of Christ, the atonement, resurrection, the church, the second coming of Christ, and Heaven.

THE STORY OF ISRAEL

The Story of Israel, as recorded in the Old Testament, may be best understood as a tragic love story about selfish desire (humans) rejecting Infinite Love (God) time after time, and time after time Infinite Love providing a new path toward reconciliation.

Clearly, the only way to know the whole story is to read the Old Testament itself; however, in this section I will provide some essential highlights of the first act or "prologue," if you will, of the full Gospel that gives the basis for the rest of the story.

The Ideal State

The Story of Israel began with God creating mankind and inviting them into an unfettered relationship with Himself: God the Father, God the Son, and God the Spirit. This is what I call "The Ideal State:" complete relational harmony between God, humanity, and creation. It is hard to imagine receiving such an invitation - an invitation to be in perfect community without brokenness, sin, or regret.

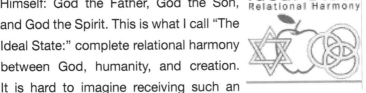

The book of Genesis provides two accounts of creation: the first is a big picture account; the second zooms in for a more detailed account of the first man and woman.

The first account is found in the first chapter of Genesis:

> Then God said, "Let us make **human beings in our image**, to be like us. **They will reign** over the fish in the sea, the birds in the sky, the livestock, all the wild animals on the earth, and the small animals that scurry along the ground." So God created human beings in his own image. In the image of God he created them;

male and female he created them. **Then God
blessed them**….

(Gen 1:26-28, NLT, emphasis mine)

God created human beings (male and female) in his image
(v.26). In this account the female and male, together as a unified
creation, are the image of God. In other words, both male and
female in perfect unity are the blessed icon (image) of God
on earth, and are commanded to multiply and oversee God's
creation together.[2]

In the Genesis 1:26–28 account, the picture of the blessed
male/female relationship is of equality and perfect harmony.
The blessing or ideal state of God's creation is relational
harmony and equality - not inferiority, one sided submission,
or dominance.[3]

Genesis 2 provides the second portrayal of the creation of the
first woman.

> He gave names to all the livestock, all the birds of the
> sky, and all the wild animals. But still there was no
> helper just right for him. So the LORD God caused the
> man to fall into a deep sleep. While the man slept, the
> LORD God took out one of the man's ribs and closed
> up the opening. Then the LORD God made a woman
> from the rib, and he brought her to the man.

---

[2] The joint image of male and female as the complete image of God can be studied more
in Paul K. Jewett, *Man as Male and Female* (Grand Rapids, MI: Eerdmans Publishing Co.,
1975).

[3] For specifics regarding the brokenness of the male psyche and its restoration to God's
design, see Richard Rohr, *From Wild Man to Wise Man* (Cincinatti, OH: St. Anthony
Messenger Press, 2005).

"At last!" the man exclaimed.

"This one is bone from my bone,
and flesh from my flesh!
She will be called 'woman,'
because she was taken from 'man.' "
(Gen 2:20-25, NLT, emphasis mine)

The name the male gives the female is the equivalent to his own; 'woman.' The account in Genesis 1 and 2 thus reveals an ideal balanced relationship between the man and the woman; two people mutually submitted to one another as they are submitted to God.

In Genesis 2 the male was made before the female, which a lot of commentary has equated with primacy. This idea really does not hold up because in the recorded progression of creation, God goes from simple to complex (water, plants, animals, and people). Now it would be reasonable to conclude by this limited scope of scripture that since the female was created after the male, the female is more complex or closer to the image of God than the male.

One thing the male's prior creation to the female does give him is the opportunity to give the female a name (Gen 2:23). In Jewish thought, the name giver is a sign of dominance. In this line of thinking, this would suggest that by the male naming his mate he had dominance over her. But, this is when it gets really cool. What is the name the male gives the female? "Woman," essentially a co-equal title.[4]

---

[4] Some scholars believe the Star of David symbol actually conveys this coequal concept, the male represented in the inverted triangle and the female in the other.

The Curse of the "I"

It wasn't until Genesis 3 that this ideal state of balance, unity, and mutual submission was disrupted by the man and woman's disobedience, which ushered in the relational curse between us

Cursed State

and God, one another, and nature. What was this disobedience? It was when the man and woman started thinking and then acting on their hidden desire: "I want to be like God."[5] And by acting upon the desire to be like God, the man and the woman destroyed the Ideal State (Perfect harmony between God, man, woman, and creation) and ushered in life under the curse, isolation and hostility as recorded in Genesis 3:16, 20-24).[6]

This scripture is an important concept to grasp in the understanding of the whole Gospel. The curse was not only a broken relationship with God but also a disruption in the ideal balance between man, woman, and His creation; "And you will desire to control your husband, but he will rule over you." It is at this point in history that the ideal state God had envisioned for His creation, having a right relationship with God and people, was lost., Tthe man becomes Adam and names the woman, Eve (a sign of broken equality), and the ground is

[5] Genesis 3:5 "God knows that your eyes will be opened as soon as you eat it, and you will be like God, knowing both good and evil."

[6] Colossians 1:21 "This includes you who were once far away from God. You were his enemies, separated from him by your evil thoughts and actions."Then he said to the woman, "I will sharpen the pain of your pregnancy, and in pain you will give birth. And you will desire to control your husband, but he will rule over you." (Gen 3:16, NLT, emphasis mine)

Genesis 3:17b ...the ground is cursed because of you. All your life you will struggle to scratch a living from it.

cursed because of their rebellion.[7]

It is often overlooked, but this curse did not only affect God's creation, but God Himself. Remember it was God's desire to exist without any barrier between Him and His creation, but because of humanity's rebellion He suffered under the curse as well. This is most easily understood by a scenario which has played itself out between every parent and every child in the history of humanity; the "I'll turn this car around right now" consequence. I have both been subject to this event and have caused this occurrence. As a child, going to a family planned trip like going to Disneyland, I have caused my parents to miss a wonderful day with their family because of my vile and sinful selfishness. But, because of the sin of "I," children never think about their parents missing out on the day, they only think about themselves. This is the sin of "I" - we don't think about how it was God's desire to live in perfect harmony with this creation. We just think about how "paradise lost" affects us.

The Promise in the Midst of the Curse

One often overlooked scripture is God's veiled promise in the midst of the curse.

While conveying the consequences of their disobedience, God promises Eve that through her the Messiah, the Savior, will be born; he who will conquer the Serpent/Satan (i.e., sin) and lift the curse.

---

[7] Then the man—Adam—named his wife Eve, because she would be the mother of all who live. ~ 23 So the LORD God banished them from the Garden of Eden, ~ to the east of the Garden of Eden. (Gen 3:20–24, NLT, emphasis mine)For insight into how the curse disrupted God's intentions for equality and respect in marriage and family, see Jeff VanVonderen, Families Where Grace Is in Place (Bloomington, MN: Bethany Publishers, 1992). For specific discussion on the toxic "control/rule" relationship of Gen. 3:16, see pages 19-23.

"He will strike your head, and you will strike his heel."
(Gen 3:15b, NLT)

It is interesting to note that God specifies that the Messiah would come from the seed of the woman and not the man—a prophecy of the virgin birth of Jesus, which was more clearly revealed by Isaiah when he wrote,

> "Look! The virgin will conceive a child! She will give birth to a son and will call him Immanuel (which means 'God is with us')" (Isa 7:14, NLT).

From this first giving of the Good News that God will restore a right relationship of His creation with Him, we learn that the Messiah was going to be the very incarnation of God, born through a woman without the seed of a man, and ultimately would defeat Satan. Additionally, this moment in history encapsulates the beauty of the relational Gospel. By God establishing "hostility" between the woman and the serpent, He establishes that even though The Fall put humanity in league with the fallen angels and Satan, God is severing that newly formed bond and laying relational claim to humanity.

Life East of Eden

Life East of Eden as recorded in the Old Testament is not only the reason for the death of Christ, but also for the Life of Christ. It is through the Old Testament narratives—which depict man and his struggles with and against God in an unflinchingly honest light—that we learn of God's unfailing love for His creation.

The Old Testament's historical and prophetic books are

tributes to our Heavenly Father's dedication and commitment to His children. He guides humanity from infancy to the point of maturation where we are able to emotionally and spiritually comprehend our need for a savior from the curse.

I sometimes feel people who have not had children are at a real disadvantage in understanding God's relationship with His creation. The metaphor of God the Father and humanity as His children is brought into so much clarity by parenthood. As parents we understand that our children have developmental stages. For example, my son, Eric loves waffles, always has. When he was just a little guy, we would cut his waffle for him and he would then happily eat his golden brown treat. When he got older there came a point where he was more than capable to cut his own waffle, but since we always did it for him, he would just ask us to cut it for him. One morning, I had made waffles for the family and he just sat there looking at his uncut waffle, when he asked, "Papa, will you please cut my waffle?" When I looked at him and said, "Dude, cut your own waffle!" Which he has ever since.

There are age appropriate levels of interaction in different stages of a child's growth. While it is unreasonable to expect a six month old baby to cut their own waffle, it is a perfectly legitimate expectation for a ten year old to cut it for themself.

The same is true with the Heavenly Father and His Children. It took time for humanity to develop to a place where we were ready for a different level of interaction with our Heavenly Father.

Ultimately, the long, complex history of Israel up to the coming of Christ is a story of God fathering and guiding humanity through the deficiencies of self-realized holiness (or self-actualization) and religion. Through the writings of scores of authors over centuries, the Old Testament makes a clear case for humanity's need for God's saving grace. This is why the Old Testament is not a collection of idealistic portraits of Jewish heroes. Of course, heroic deeds mark some of the more memorable passages. But as a whole, the Old Testament books are characterized by an honest representation of man as he is: living East of Eden, in desperate need of a savior.

GOING
DEEPER

BREAKING GROUND

What is an event or season in your life that has defined who you are in the present?

Why is this event/season so important to understanding who you are now?

How does this event/season influence the decisions you make today?

THE DIG

Read Hebrews 11:39-40

What is the biggest promise someone has ever made to you? Was it fulfilled? Why or why not?

How do you view the Old Testament as it relates to your Christian faith?

Read Luke 1:30-38

Why was the Old Testament important to Mary, Mother of Jesus?

Without her knowledge of the Old Testament prophecies, how do you think Mary would have responded to the angel telling her she was pregnant?

Why is the Old Testament important to your Christian faith?

What are some Old Testament verses that have helped you in your faith?

How have these Old Testament scriptures strengthened your faith?

Read Isaiah 53:1-5

How do you see Jesus in this prophecy?

Read 1 Peter 2:24 and Matthew 8:17

How did the first century church view the Old Testament?

GETTING OUT OF THE HOLE

If you are new to the Old Testament, it can be an overwhelming collection of books to approach for the first time. Fear not. The Old Testament is composed of groupings of writing: The Pentateuch (first five books of the Bible), The Histories, The Major Prophets, and the Minor Prophets. Take some time to familiarize yourself with some of the following resources to help you better understand the Old Testament.

SUPPORTING RESOURCES

Here are a few suggestions for continued study:

Youngblood, Ronald. *The Heart of the Old Testament*. Grand Rapids, MI: Baker Books, 1998.

Matthews, Victor. *Old Testament Turning Points*. Grand Rapids, MI: Baker Academic, 2005.

http://www.patheos.com/blogs/jesuscreed/2013/04/24/you-might-have-a-soterian-gospel-if-you/

Most Bibles have cross-references (guides in the center column or at the bottom of your page, which show you other places in the Bible where the same truth/reference is communicated); begin exploring some of these references and broaden your context for what God has been communicating across the generations.

SYMBOL TWO:
THE LIFE OF CHRIST

THE LIFE OF CHRIST

> "It is not that God's help and presence must still be proved in our life; rather God's presence and help have been demonstrated for us in the life of Jesus Christ. It is in fact more important for us to know what God did to Israel, in God's Son Jesus Christ, than to discover what God intends for us today. The fact that Jesus Christ died is more important than the fact that I will die. And the fact that Jesus Christ was raised from the dead is the sole ground of my hope that I, too, will be raised on the day of judgment"
>
> - Dietrich Bonhoeffer, *Life Together and Prayerbook of the Bible*

Symbol Explanation: XP

The Chi Rho is one of the oldest symbols of the Christian faith. Constantine, the emperor of the Roman Empire, made the Chi Rho famous when he adopted it as a prominent symbol at the start of his imperial reign. It is formed by superimposing the first two (capital) letters chi (X) and rho (P) of the Greek word, ΧΡΙΣΤΟΣ (Christ). In the previous chapter, I mentioned that the word "Christ" in the Greek language is the same Hebrew word translated "Messiah," thus connecting Jesus and the life He lived, with the promised Messiah of the Old Testament prophecies.

Why did Jesus live?

Ironically, perhaps one of the most difficult things for salvationists (Soterians) to fit into their theology is the life of Jesus. This may seem like a funny thing to say, but the reality is for those who only focus on salvation, there is no real reason for the life of Christ outside of His death on the cross.[8]

So why did Jesus come and live and not just come to die?

Seemingly this question has the potential for great theological debate, but the fact is that Jesus was very clear about why he came and lived. In fact, Scripture records seven different times when Jesus answers the question of why He came. Over the next several pages we will read into Jesus answer the question of why He came.

Fulfillment

"Life is a promise, fulfill it." -Mother Teresa

His first answer is found in Matthew 5:17, when Jesus said, "Don't misunderstand why I have come. I did not come to abolish the law of Moses or the writings of the prophets. **No, I came to accomplish their purpose.**"

Here, Jesus is making the connection that was made in the previous chapter, that the Story of Israel is an essential part of the Gospel narrative. With great clarity, Jesus, is explicitly stating that one of the reasons He came was to fulfill the purpose of the Law and messianic prophecies of the Jewish prophets.

Let's be honest, the Law of Moses and Old Testament prophecies can be very confusing for a 21st century Christian;

---

[8] It's no coincidence that Paul states in Romans 5:10 that we are "saved by His life."

in fact, there probably is not a week that goes by that I, as a pastor, am not asked about some obscure law of the Old Testament. Some of the more frequently asked questions about the 613 laws of Moses concern marginal issues, like tattoos (Leviticus 19:28), earrings (Hosea 2:13), and Christmas trees (Jeremiah 10:3-4).

Perhaps the most significant question I'm asked is whether or not we must adhere to the Old Testament Law.

Jesus directly answers this general question through His statement that He came to accomplish the purpose of the law. But what is the "purpose of the law"?

This question leads to the essential question on biblical interpretation: How does each passage of scripture help begin, build, or restore a right relationship with God and/or people? Every law can be understood through that lens.

(I will expand this system of biblical interpretation more in depth in Symbol Three: the Cross.)

Ultimately, the Law, was not something given as a path to self-realized holiness in order for a person to be accepted by God. No, the Law was given to show humanity their need of a Savior to offer relational reconciliation through grace (Romans 5:20).

Service

> "The best way to find yourself is to lose yourself in the service of others." — Mahatma Gandhi

Another reason Jesus came is found in Mark 10:45:

> "For even the Son of Man came not to be served but to serve others and to give his life as a ransom for many."
> (Mark 10:45, NLT)

> *"The best way to find yourself is to lose yourself in the service of others."*
> *-Mahatma Gandhi*

I am always struck by the stunning humility of this statement. It is the great paradox of divine authority: the Creator came to serve His creation (Col. 1:16-17).

Now Jesus was not opposed to being served (i.e. the woman pouring perfume on his feet), but that is not why he came. He came to serve us by paying our sin ransom of eternal separation from God: death. And as we will see in John 12:27, this was no small price to pay.

Payment

While talking to Andrew and Philip about the inevitable violent crescendo of his ministry and in palpable distress, Jesus prays,

> "Now my soul is deeply troubled. Should I pray, 'Father, save me from this hour'? But this is the very reason I came!" (John 12:27, NLT)

Why was Jesus' soul deeply troubled? I think most would say it was because He was facing the cruelty of crucifixion, one of the most brutal forms of capital punishment humans have conceived. But was Jesus' soul really deeply troubled because of the physical pain he was certain to endure, or was it something else, something much worse?

Let me propose a different view of Jesus' troubled soul: perhaps Jesus was suffering from what today we might call, "separation anxiety."

Think about it, Jesus for all eternity had been in perfect fellowship with the Holy Trinity. What is holy cannot be joined with anything/one with any impurities. So, when Jesus took on the sins of the world, He was expelled from perfect community and seamless unity into complete isolation to pay the price of the His creation's rebellion.

Jesus knew this excruciating reality before He came, knew it while He served us, and He still willingly paid our debt. (This will be explored in more depth in the next chapter, The Cross.)

A Light in the Darkness

> "Darkness cannot drive out darkness: only light can do that. Hate cannot drive out hate: only love can do that."
> - Martin Luther King, Jr.

Light makes the most impact in the dark. During Christmas time we don't go look at Christmas lights at noon, rather, we wait until it is dark. On the 4th of July, we don't watch fireworks at 11AM, no, we also wait until it is dark. Why? The answer is simple: light makes the most impact in the dark. Christians are people of the Light.

The missionary John Keith Falconer said, "I have but one candle of life to burn, and I would rather burn it out in a land filled with darkness than in a land flooded with light."

Jesus came to light the path in this dark world leading toward having a right relationship with God and people. Those who choose to walk this illuminated path are also enlightened to the sacred calling of carrying Christ's light to others. As he proclaimed, "I have come as a light to shine in this dark world, so that all who put their trust in me will no longer remain in the dark." (John 12:46, NLT)

At our church we symbolize this high calling of illumination at baptism gatherings by giving each person who is being baptized a large cylindrical candle with three wicks. For us, this candle represents someone's Gospel story: the unlit candle represents someone's life, full of the potential for light. However, unless someone shares their light with the person, they remain in the dark.

During the gathering we ask the person being baptized, who was significant in their faith journey, i.e., who shared their light with him/her? We then invite those identified to light that person's candle, symbolizing this transfer of light and his/her answering to the call to be the Light in a dark place.

Break the Caste

Unhealthy people make themselves feel better by pointing out other people's flaws. It is the classic bully syndrome so frequently discussed in the American school system today.

In Matthew 9, Jesus is confronted by some religious bullies who ask a hostile question intended to tear Jesus and his followers

> *Jesus proclaims through His life that all people matter to God...*

down:

"Why does your teacher eat with such scum?" When Jesus heard this, he said, "Healthy people don't need a doctor—sick people do." Then he added, "Now go and learn the meaning of this Scripture: 'I want you to show mercy, not offer sacrifices.' For I have come to call not those who think they are righteous, but those who know they are sinners." (Matt 9:11b-13, NLT)

This is the biblical response to religious bullying: truth drives out half-truth, light drives out darkness.

The world segments people into groups according to perceived value. My wife and I like to watch Downton Abbey. It is interesting to me the emphasis on the characters' pride in not being viewed as lower on the social ladder. The aristocrats are glad they are not servants; the head butler is pretentious about not being a valet; the valet is pompous about not being a footman—and on and on.

Perhaps one of the most egregious real world examples of this is found in India, as illustrated by the current manifestation of their caste system, which still separates people into a hierarchy of human society.

One of the profound purposes of Christ's life is to break the spiritual and relational castes. He proclaims through his life that all people matter to God, that He loves them and wants to invite them into an unfettered and restored relationship with Him.

Invitation

> "I know at that moment what he's given me and it isn't
> a chair. It's an invitation, a welcome, the knowledge
> that I am accepted here. He hasn't given me a place to
> sit. He's given me a place to belong."
> — Katja Millay, *The Sea of Tranquility*

In Mark 1:38 Jesus communicated another crucial reason for coming:

"We must go on to other towns as well, and I will preach to them, too. That is why I came."

So, what exactly did Jesus come to preach?

He came to proclaim that the Son of God did not come to perpetuate a religious, political, or social system, but to invite people to belong.

Jesus announced to a lost world that He came as the incarnation of the Gospel, that He is the Good News made flesh, a literal fulfillment of the Genesis 3:15 promise. No longer does mankind need to live East of Eden, but the LORD has come to crush the serpent's head of isolation with the heel of love.

We followers of Jesus are intended to take up this purpose, to be the invitation, carrying the same message of forgiveness and inclusion to a world lost in condemnation and isolation.

Clarity

> "One should use common words to say
> uncommon things." — Arthur Schopenhauer

Clarity is a difficult thing. Often it's not the inability to express oneself; it's the lack of courage that's the problem. Many times, people are not clear because they simply do not want to be clear; the cost is too high. Some avoid direct, clear truth by using clever sentence structure. Others parse the meaning of simple words (like "is") as illustrated by former President Bill Clinton during the Monica Lewinsky scandal.

In Matthew 10, Jesus brings a lot of clarity in His final "why I came" statement:

"Don't imagine that I came to bring peace to the earth! I came not to bring peace, but a sword." (Matt 10:34, NLT)

Many have a hard time with this statement, but fully devoted followers of Christ eventually must wrestle with what Jesus means. What you'll find is rather surprising! Christ's divisive statement actually offers those willing to examine His life a path to relational wholeness with God and people.

In my personal theological wrestling match with Christ's paradigm-altering statement, I have found this claim to only make sense in light of the concept of restored relationship. Whenever I don't understand a passage, I ask myself, "How does it begin, build, or restore a right relationship with God or people?" Well let's ask this question of Jesus' difficult statement.

One thing I have learned as a pastor over the years is that clarity almost inevitably leads to both reconciliation and conflict. When someone speaks the truth clearly, it brings some people together-but it also, more often than not, creates conflict.

For example, this scenario usually plays out when a wedding engagement is announced. Inevitably, some welcome the news, while others find reason for dissent. The engagement is a metaphorical sword dividing the couple's community.

This is the same metaphorical sword Jesus is talking about in His statement above. By Jesus' clear declaration that He is the blessing in the midst of the curse, He forces people to choose: either He is the incarnation of the promise or a false prophet come to deceive.

Remember that the Messiah, although being God, willingly came into a broken and messy world—a world that initiated the curse of relational brokenness—a world in which some people may choose isolation rather than restoration. This separation, although not the desire of our Creator, is made possible because relationship without choice is bondage.

The Illuminating Life

Jesus' life can be very difficult to interpret when not equipped with the right questions to ask or cultural context through which to filter it.

It is crucial to resist jumping to conclusions using our own cultural contexts when interpreting the life of Jesus. Instead, we must take the time to see Him first through the Story of Israel.

This is a primary reason that Jesus came to live and not just to die. As he walked this earth, he brought a transformational illumination to everyone he encountered. The life that He shared reflected the beauty of relational wholeness with God and people, a life illuminating the timeless story of God's love. His life had that power, not only for those who followed Him during His temporal ministry, but for those of us who seek to follow Him as fully surrendered disciples of XP, Jesus Christ.

GOING
DEEPER

BREAKING GROUND

Share about someone who has been instrumental or a mentor in your life.

What key lessons have they taught you about living a rich and satisfying life?

THE DIG

In your opinion, why was it important for Jesus to live for over thirty years, have an impactful ministry, and build personal relationships—and not just come to die?

What do you believe is the most important teaching that we learn from Jesus' life?

What does Jesus' life teach you about service? (Mark 10:45)

What does Jesus' life teach you about how to be a light in the darkness? (John 12:46)

"Darkness cannot drive out darkness: only light can do that.
Hate cannot drive out hate: only love can do that."
-Martin Luther King, Jr.

How does Dr. King's statement clarify being a Christian light?

What does Jesus' life teach you about loving others? (Luke 10:25-37)

What does Jesus' life teach you about living a life of invitation? (Mark 1: 38)

How does clarity strengthen relationships? (p. 47-49) (Matthew 10:34)

What is one of the more difficult examples in Christ's life for you to implement in your own life?

GETTING OUT OF THE HOLE

You need others to help you. Find those who care about your growth and seek out wisdom on how to invite people to journey with you in your goals. Create space in your life to do the same for others.

What is one step you can take this week to move toward living that difficult teaching/example out?

Is this something you need others to help you with? If so, who can you ask to help you and what role can they play?

SUPPORTING RESOURCES

Here are a few suggestions for continued study:

Yancey, Philip. *The Jesus I Never Knew*. Grand Rapids, MI: Zondervan, 2008.

Wright, N.T. *Simply Jesus*. New York, NY: Harper One, 2011.

NOTES. YOUR THOUGHTS. PERSONAL APPLICATION.

SYMBOL THREE:
THE CROSS

WHY DID JESUS DIE

"At the center of the Christian faith lies a picture. Christian art and architecture, literature and hymns, are dominated by the symbol of the cross. A symbol, however, both invites and demands thought and reflection. What are we to make of this symbol? What does it tell us about God and the world, or about our nature and ultimate destiny? Why is it that at the center of a faith in a loving God lies a symbol of death and despair-the dreadful picture of a man dying through crucifixion?"

-Alister E. McGrath, *The Mystery of the Cross* (Zondervan, 1988)

Symbol Explanation: The Cross

Since at least the 2nd century, in both visual depictions, and in the gesture of making the sign, Christians have used the Cross as a shorthand for their faith.[10] In fact, the use of the symbol was so prominent early in the Christian church, that some of the Church Fathers had to defend Christians against charges of being worshippers of the Cross. Beyond the obvious direct reference to the method of execution of Christ, many have pointed to the symbol's possible reference to Christ's Great Commandment—to love God and one's neighbor as oneself (Matt 22:37-39)—through the simultaneously vertical (God) and horizontal (man) nature of the symbol.

---

[10]For more, see the New Advent Catholic Encyclopedia's entry: "Sign of the Cross."

The Cross in Context

We have now arrived, in my opinion, at the most misunderstood symbol in the Christian faith: the symbol of Christ's sacrificial death on a Roman Cross.

Let me start by saying I am (quite literally) eternally grateful for Jesus dying on the Cross to pay for my sins and the sins of the world; it is through this act that I can someday be in eternal, unfettered fellowship with God the Father, God the Son, and God the Holy Spirit.

That being said, much of Western Christianity has taken the Cross and turned it into something it was not intended to be: the whole story, the whole Gospel. An example from popular culture: Just as *Stars Wars Episode 4: A New Hope* (the original 1978 film) is not the complete six-part Star Wars saga, the Cross is not the whole story. The Cross is certainly an integral part of the Gospel—the turning point in fact—but it is not the Gospel in its complete and redemptive entirety.

The Cross is absolutely essential to the Christian faith, but without knowing the Story of Israel and the Life of Christ, we do not have the context to fully understand the cross's significance. And what follows is equally necessary. Without the resurrection, the cross is meaningless (I'll unpack this statement in Symbol Four: The Resurrection, so put down your stones), and the church's hope of the second coming and Infinite Love (everlasting life in the unfettered presence of God) is without justification.

The Significance of the Cross

So in the full context of the Gospel, what is the significance of the Cross?

To understand this, we need to start with another question: Who is God? Ask ten people and get ten different answers. Who really knows? The inherent impossibility of describing an infinite, omnipresent, omnipotent, omni-etc., being granted up front, let's wade into the marshy swamp of theology for a moment by attempting to (at least partially) answer this rather daunting question.

If you went to Sunday school (worst marketing name ever), you may have a Pavlovian response to this question and answered, "God is love."

Good answer. But what does it actually mean?

Let me step back a space and riddle you this: What is required for love to exist? (Insert Jeopardy music here...) For love to exist, you must have more than one person or conscious being. At the bare minimum there needs to be at least two who are in relationship. In this way, the very fact that "God is love" means God is a God of relationship.

Here's the rub. If God is love, who was He in relationship with before He created anyone or anything?

You may think, well maybe He became love once He created the earth, but there is a problem with that: God is the same today as He was before time. So if God is love, He has always been love, and we know the prerequisite of love is having someone to love.

The Inherently Relational God

So, who was God in relationship with before creation? The answer is Himself. This is the essence of the mystery of the Trinity.

God is in relationship with Himself because God is a relational God. God is made up of three persons: the Father, Son, and Holy Spirit. They are eternal and existing as one in perfect love and relationship.

God cannot be understood outside of love and love is nonexistent outside of relationship. Therefore, God cannot be comprehended outside of the context of relationship.

Just as God is love, God is also "relationship." In fact, everything about God is relational; if it is not relational, it is not of God.

Nothing God created is in isolation. This is true on both a

micro and a macro level. From the interconnectedness of protons and electrons, to planetary gravitational balance, all of revealed creation depends upon, affects, and interrelates with other aspects of creation. Whether it be quantum physics or metaphysics, God has built a universe around relationships.

If this is true, then it should radically change how we read Scripture. If all things of God are relational, then in order to understand God's instruction to us in the Bible, we must first discover how it builds our relationship with Him and/or others.

My default guide in understanding and applying scripture is asking the question, "How does this instruction begin, build, or restore a right relationship with God and/or people?"

I believe this is the key question to proper understanding and application of all scripture. The next time you are perplexed with the meaning or purpose of a scripture, try asking this question: "How does this instruction begin, build, or restore a right relationship with God and/or people?"

Relational Space

Relationship creation, relationship building, and relationship restoration is the central theme throughout Scripture. From the very first chapter of Genesis, to the culmination of the story of God in Revelation, we have the story of relationship creation, building, and restoration.

Let's look back at the creation account once again through this relational grid. What is God creating? He is creating a complex universe and terrestrial ecosystem that is in perfect relationship and harmony.

The one thing God did not originally create with a relational connection, He declared to be "not good": "It is not good for the man to be alone. I will make a helper who is just right for him." (Gen 2:18, NLT, emphasis mine)

Did God make a mistake? Or was He giving Adam relational space to discover the perfect design of interdependent relationships? Did God knowingly create a less-than-ideal existence for Adam just to allow him the relational space to observe and recognize his need for a human partnership, like those he observed in the rest of creation?

If the reason for the delay was to give Adam relational space to discover this relational need on his own, then God exhibited perfect and selfless love, which would be an example of perfect relationship.

It has always amazed me to witness the maturity of those who are secure enough in their own beliefs to give someone else the relational space to discover truth on their own. I have been afforded this relational space on several occasions in my life and, in turn, intentionally try to offer it to others.

At our church, I call baptism Sundays "The best day ever." And in terms of what we gather together as a church body to experience, I mean it. The reason I love baptism Sundays so much is because we spend time hearing the stories of the persons being baptized, meeting those who have been significant in his/her/their faith journeys, and celebrating with them as they are baptized.

Above all though, the story of every individual who stands in front of our church on those Sundays is the story of relational reconciliation with God-and a microcosm of the greater story of God's restoration of mankind to Himself. It is the one story I will never tire of hearing.

You never know what you are going to get on one of our baptism Sundays. You have the combination of a minefield of theological, societal, and psychological uncertainty and a pastor who has the social graces of an ox. One thing is for sure in this volatile combination of spiritual tension: it is going to be interesting.

One Sunday, I was interviewing a new follower of Christ who was taking his next step of faith by being baptized. During the conversation he started talking about his previous lives... When he finished sharing about his adventures in other times and bodies, I sheepishly asked him, "So, do you here in this place and time proclaim Jesus Christ as your Lord and Savior?" He replied with a resounding, "Yes!" With a collective sigh of relief, we all applauded.

The next day I had a very perturbed church attendee confront me about not correcting the, let's say, unorthodox theology of the previous day's baptiz-ee.

I asked him, "Has your faith been damaged?"

"Of course not, my faith is solid," he replied, clearly offended.

And so I asked, "Was your faith always so strong?"

"No."

"Then how did your faith become so solid?"

"By spending time in the Word and going to church," he stated; this time the offense had given way to pride.

"Then perhaps we should afford him the same relational space you were given."

Allowance for relational space to grow requires a long-term view of relationships. It does not require adherence to a certain list of rules or doctrines, only relational pliability a willingness to expand and grow into the person God has envisioned you to be.

This makes a lot of Christians nervous. They think if you allow relational space for growth, people will start erecting golden calves. Of course I am not advocating for a free-for-all theology where every answer is the right answer. What I am proposing is an organic, relational growth track whose primary objective is promoting a right relationship with God and a right relationship with people. This requires trusting that the Spirit of God is working with/within/through people in the midst of imperfect spiritual understanding and lifestyles.

The Three Holies

"Holy" is one of those Christian words that is thrown around a lot, but profoundly misunderstood and mis-used. This really isn't the fault of English speakers because the English translations use "holy" to cover multiple more nuanced words.

One meaning of the word holy is attributed to God, as in "God is holy!" (This is the Hebrew word, qadosh). In this use of the word, holy is defined as sacred or absolutely pure.

However the word, holy in English is a homograph (words that are spelled the same but have different meanings) and the dual meaning confuses a lot of people. The other definition of the word, holy is: "being set apart for God's purpose" (this is the Hebrew word, qodesh). An example of this is found in Exodus 26:34, "Then put the Ark's cover—the place of atonement—on top of the Ark of the Covenant inside the Most Holy Place."

The use of holy place here is not a proclamation that a certain place is absolutely pure, only that it is a designated place set aside for God's purpose, and as a result is to be kept as pure as possible.

And just to completely confuse the concept of holy, some English Bibles translate the Greek word ἁγιασμός (pronounced: hag-ee-as-mos), which means, refinement also as "holy." An example of this is found in 1 Peter 1:2:

> "God the Father knew you and chose you long ago,
> and his Spirit has made you holy." (Peter 1:2, NLT)

The distinction between these three uses of the word is important because holy (qadosh) tells us something about God that is essential in the formulation of our faith; God is absolutely pure and without fault, meaning we can trust Him explicitly and without reservation. We can accept our designation of being holy/set apart (*qodesh*) without fear because we know we serve a holy/absolutely pure (*qadosh*) God. Finally, because we are holy/being refined (ἁγιασμός), we can come to God without fear of rejection because refinement is part of His plan.

Love Lost

I hate the English word "love."

OK, hate might be a slight overstatement, but I do often find myself cringing at the shotgun (mis)use of "love." In short, I take issue with the culturally diminished form of the word. How it is often used in the present English vernacular has important (one might argue eternal) ramifications. Why? Our diminished application of "love" has fostered a diminished view of God.

If "God is love" and our understanding of love is framed by our cultural use of the word, then we're left with a badly warped view of the very essence of God. We say we "love" just about everything-most of the time temporal, frivolous things. TV shows, movies, and songs, all of which we inevitably dismiss for something newer.

A (soon to be dated) example: While writing this book, I heard a young lady say she loved the current number one song "Call Me Maybe." Now, I don't need to be a prophet to correctly predict that by the time you read this book, most teenie-boppers will no longer declare their "love" for "Call Me Maybe." In fact, it is more likely that you will find spoofs openly mocking it on Reddit than diehard teens "liking" it on Facebook.

While this is an obviously loose, and seemingly harmless use of the word, the reality is that our continued collective misuse of "love" subconsciously erodes our understanding of God. So, if God is love and our subconscious concept of love is trendy songs, blockbuster movies, and reality TV shows that are disregarded as soon as something new comes out, then for the love of God, no wonder people are ambivalent about accepting and responding to God and His love.

Fortunately, the understanding of love can be assisted by the previous discussion on holiness or absolute purity.

We know God is holy, so we know His love must be absolutely pure. This is quite unlike the temporal love portrayed in teenie bopper music that we delete from our iPods after a few months. No, it is love in its ideal state.

So, what is love in its ideal state?

LOVE IS...
- patient
- kind
- joyous in truth
- unrelenting
- faithful
- always hopeful
- enduring forever

For the answer we turn to 1 Corinthians 13, also known as the "love chapter." Here we have a list of what constitutes holy and godly love. Go through the following list and see if the current cultural use of the word love is consistent with God's standard of love.

Clearly the kind of "love" used to describe one's feelings for a pop song is lacking in all categories of this description.

The common romantic misuse of "love" is more detrimental still.

A few years ago a famous actor had an affair with a famous actress (shocking, I know). The actress had been married for almost a decade and had children with her husband (also a famous actor, by the way).

When the adulterous male actor was confronted about the marriage-ending affair on a talk show, his answer was enlightening:

"I didn't plan to fall in love with her, you know. It just happened... I chose to walk toward love instead of walk away from it."

What kind of "love" is he talking about? Patient love? Clearly not. Kind love? Not on the husband's and children's side. Joyous in truth? Whose truth? Certainly not faithful and enduring love (their adulterous relationship lasted only two years).

The current cultural definition of "love" is a cheap imitation (if even that) of a genuine, holy, and godly love. Godly love transcends all understanding and can transform even the direst of conditions.

A Powerful Submission

So often the Christian church has tried to exert dominance over the culture in which it finds itself placed, but the Cross is a powerful challenge to the desire for dominance.

The Cross is a symbol of submission.

When a Christian looks upon the symbol of the cross, it is a reminder that an omni-powerful God willingly submitted Himself to atone for the depravity of His creation. The cross truly symbolizes the passion (willingness to suffer) of Christ. This passion illustrates that there is nothing God will allow to separate us from Him and the price He is willing to pay in order to achieve relational wholeness. Consequently, the symbol of the cross is a constant challenge to the sinful allure of apathy that is so prevalent in the 21st century church. For it is the symbol of the cross that reminds humanity, in the simplicity of one vertical beam and one horizontal beam, that Christians must daily pick up their cross and follow Jesus to selfless sacrifice.

Every time the cross is sung about, worn, or referenced, it requires the Christian to reflect: "How am I dying to myself and being remade into the symbol of Infinite Love?"

It is this love that persists through every adverse situation, trial, and hurt. It is the access to Infinite Love that warms the soul when the chill of darkness threatens to snuff out hope.

The Perfect Weakness

Several years ago, at another baptism Sunday, a young woman in her twenties began sharing her story. It was one of those stories that demolished one of my preconceived notions of how God demonstrates His love.

She shared that as a child her single mom would have a string of boyfriends who would come and go. Finally, when she was five years old, her mom met a man that came but wouldn't go. He moved into their lives. And that was when the nightmare began.

Shortly after this newly formed family was patched together, she was exposed to an explosive mix of drugs and cult-like religious fanaticism. It wasn't long before this five-year-old girl realized that even a small accident, like spilling her milk, was punishable by a beating.

As we sat there on handmade copper pipe stools in front of her community, she shared the terrifying reality of her childhood. She recounted how she was made to stand in the middle of the room after she had an accident and, in a sick ritual cloaked as a religious ceremony, they would attempt to beat the demon that caused her imperfection, her sin, out of her. To make things worse, during these "exorcisms" her mother would yell at her that God hated her.

It was at this point in the story that I learned a powerful lesson about the depth of God's love and the length that He will go through to make sure we experience it. She said, that every time her mother told her God hated her, she heard a voice envelope her, assuring her, "It is not true, I love you."

This was not a little girl who was raised in a Christian church singing "Jesus Loves Me" every week in Sunday school. She had never been told about the love of God, only the vengeance of God; yet that did not stop God from expressing His love for her.

God's love cannot be contained in a formula or restricted to a building with a steeple on top. There is no place or situation God's love cannot penetrate, persevere, and transform. God has shown a perfect weakness to the enemy: His endless love for His creation. This perfect weakness was exposed by the cross which was ultimately conquered by His love.

Relational Separation/Relational Restoration

It has been my observation as a pastor that the true magnitude of the sacrifice Christ made on the Cross has not been fully realized by many Christians because of the overwhelming physical suffering that Jesus experienced on the Cross. I am not trying to minimize the pain and suffering Jesus experienced through His beatings and crucifixion; however, the more profound pain Jesus experienced was most likely relational rather than physical.

Christ willingly went to the Cross, which meant for the first time He would be severed from the Holy (*qadosh*/absolutely pure) Trinity because He would take on our sin and brokenness; sin and brokenness which are by their very nature incompatible with absolute purity and wholeness. For this reason it is a mistake to solely focus on the physical beating and punishment Christ underwent during the crucifixion. The more severe suffering was the complete separation from the perfect community Christ had known for all eternity. It was perhaps this separation that caused Jesus' true anguish; he expressed the profound pain of taking on the sins of the world when he exclaimed the Davidic Psalm, "My God, my God why have you forsaken me?"

We know love because God, who is love, revealed Himself to us. God is love, so as previously discussed in this chapter, God is relationship-a perfect expression of love in community. It is through this understanding of His perfect love that we can begin to understand the significance of the Cross.

GOING
DEEPER

BREAKING GROUND

Who is your favorite redemptive character or hero from a movie or popular story?

What qualities in that character do you find most admirable?

THE DIG

So, in the full context of the Gospel, what is the significance of the Cross? (p. 49)

Who is God?

Read 1 John 4:8,16

If "God is love," what does that tell us about the importance of relationship to God?

How does this relationship relate to the concept of the Trinity?

Would you agree or disagree with the following statement from page 51: "Just as God is love, God is also "relationship." In fact, everything about God is relational; if it is not relational, it is not of God."

How does the Cross inspire us to begin, build, or restore relationships with God and others?

How has God given you the relational space to experience His love?

How have you offered relational space to others in their growth?

If the Cross represents sacrificial love and Christ calls us to pick up our cross daily, how are you intentionally living out sacrificial love?

What do you believe was the greater suffering for Jesus during his crucifixion: physical or emotional?

Why do you think the first time Jesus cried out during His crucifixion was when He took the sins of the world? (Matthew 27:46)

GETTING OUT OF THE HOLE

What's one way you can offer someone close to you more relational space to grow spiritually or experience God's love?

What are three ways this week you can show sacrificial love to someone by living out the full expression of God's love He has shown you?

SUPPORTING RESOURCES

Here are a few suggestions for continued study:

Baker, Mark and Green, Joel. *Recovering the Scandal of the Cross.* Downers Grove, IL: InterVarsity Press, 2000.

Beilby, James and Eddy, Paul, eds. *The Nature of the Atonement: Four Views*. Downers Grove, IL: IVP Academic, 2006.

NOTES. YOUR THOUGHTS. PERSONAL APPLICATION.

SYMBOL FOUR:
THE EMPTY TOMB

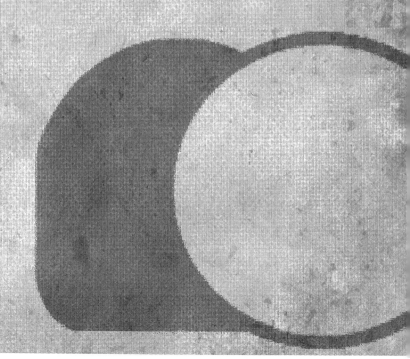

THE EMPTY TOMB

> "If Jesus rose from the dead, then you have to accept
> all that he said; if he didn't rise from the dead, then why
> worry about any of what he said? The issue on which
> everything hangs is not whether or not you like his
> teaching but whether or not he rose from the dead."
> - Timothy Keller, *The Reason for God: Belief in an Age
> of Skepticism*

Symbol Explanation: The Empty Tomb

The symbol of the Empty Tomb
appears in many Christian images,
from Medieval stained glass and
relief sculptures, to Renaissance
oil paintings, to modern day
inspirational screensavers. While the
representations of the tomb vary, most

portray the tomb as an above ground walk-in tomb, while others
depict it as a free-standing crypt. Despite the differences, all of
these depictions share one miraculous detail: the emphasis on
the emptiness of the tomb that once held the deceased body
of Christ.

> "And if Christ has not been raised, then your faith is
> useless and you are still guilty of your sins."
> (1 Corinthians 15:17, NLT)

The Resurrection Justified the Cross

The Resurrection validates Christ's sacrifice on the Cross
through His victory over death (which is the result of sin).
Without the Resurrection, Christ's death on the Cross would

have been the end of the story, and the end of the fledgling faith movement. It was the Resurrection that transformed eleven fearful disciples into eleven fearless apostles who ultimately turned the world upside-down.

In the Empty Tomb the greatest paradox mankind has ever known presents itself: in the eyes of the world, the pathway to true life looks like death. What the world perceives as the inevitable, natural end of the story is in God's paradoxical design, the beginning.

The Apostle Paul touched on this paradox in Colossians 3: "For you died to this life, and your real life is hidden with Christ in God" (Col 3:3, NLT).

Perhaps another interpretation could be: By laying down your life in the (metaphoric) tomb of Christ, you will find the secret to life.

Jesus, facing his crucifixion, explains this paradox by using an earthly illustration:

> "I tell you the truth, unless a kernel of wheat is planted in the soil and dies, it remains alone. But its death will produce many new kernels—a plentiful harvest of new lives. Those who love their life in this world will lose it. Those who care nothing for their life in this world will keep it for eternity. Anyone who wants to be my disciple must follow me, because my servants must be where I am. And the Father will honor anyone who serves me." (John 12:23–26)

This declaration to His disciples—that they must follow Him into the metaphoric tomb by dying to themselves—must have been shocking, even terrifying. They were expecting a temple… not a tomb.[11]

The False Paths: Self-Realized Holiness & Religion

I believe Jesus' teaching on the narrow road is one of the most misunderstood concepts of the Gospel; at the very least, there is a widespread lack in understanding of the full magnitude of Jesus' words in Matthew 7:13–14.

Jesus makes it very clear that sin (anything less than God's perfect vision for our lives) is a barrier that separates us from our Holy (absolutely pure) God, because what is not absolutely pure cannot be part of what is Holy.

The blocks of this biblically described sin barrier are made up of "cheap grace,"[12] self-actualization, self-realized holiness, and religion. While popular conceptions might quickly identify the seven deadly sins—lust, gluttony, greed, sloth, wrath, envy, pride—many, including many Christians, do not recognize both self-realized holiness and religion as barriers. It perhaps might sound right and good that we should try to make ourselves holy (absolutely pure). However, in so doing, we are only trying to make ourselves worthy of God through our own efforts, a goal

---

[11] The term "kenosis" is sometimes used in theological circles to describe this idea. The "emptying" of God into Jesus for the purpose of raising Him back to life also raises us to life. So, God's love is expressed in vulnerability, sacrifice and death before resurrection brings life. Phil. 2:5-11 gives us a great summary of how this works. For further reading, see William Placher, *Narratives of a Vulnerable God* (Louisville, KY: Westminster John Knox Press, 1994). For a view of God's vunerability throughout the Old Testament, see Terence Fretheim, *The Suffering God: An Old Testament Perspective* (Philadelphia, PA: Fortress Press, 1994).

[12] I'm borrowing the term ("cheap grace") from my favorite theologian, Dietrick Bonhoffer. If you haven't read his *The Cost of Discipleship*, I highly recommend it.

that is grounded in pride and thus, has positioned many not on the true path to life, but rather on the highway to hell.

It's not surprising that the twin idols of self-realized holiness and religion (man-made path to God) have become acceptable substitutes in many faith communities. Certainly righteousness and religiosity are admirable pursuits... Right?

The more subtle the deception, the more destructive its possibilities.

The lure of self-realized holiness is a big reason why I believe Jesus clearly states that few will ever find the gateway to life. The pursuit of holiness has all the superficial trappings of the right path, but it is not the Gospel.

The Gospel's predominant theme is the centrality of Christ as our Leader and Savior, that Jesus, and Jesus alone, must be on the throne of our lives. We "must worship no other gods, for the Lord, whose very name is Jealous, is a God who is jealous about his relationship with you" (Exodus 34:14, NLT).

This assertion of God's centrality—to the point of eclipsing all competition—is reiterated throughout the story of God.

Most Christians would agree that Exodus 34:14 is clear in its utter rejection of the worship of the gods of other religions. Perhaps it may also be true that most Christians have even made the connection that work, sports, and even our children, can potentially be "other gods" or idols. But few Christians have run the chain far enough to realize that the link of religion or the pursuit of self-realized holiness can be every bit as much of a false god as a hand-carved idol.

The Pharisees made this grievous error and Jesus exposed it when He said,

> "You hypocrites! Isaiah was right when he prophesied about you, for he wrote, 'These people honor me with their lips, but their hearts are far from me. Their worship is a farce, for they teach man-made ideas as commands from God.'" (Matt 15:7-9, NLT)

The True Path: The Narrow Road

The path to life is narrow and flanked by terminally deep gorges on either side. To live an extraordinary life while not becoming prideful, remote, or hypocritical, is indeed a narrow way.
To confess Jesus as your Lord and Savior, and then to actually submit to His teaching is indeed a narrow way.

To accept the unmerited gift of grace while not judging others is indeed the narrow way.

To proclaim Christ's power before the forces of darkness armed only with peace and love is indeed the narrow way.[13]

The narrow path is treacherous and full of peril; and, ironically, the longer people are on the path, the more easily they can lose their way. There's only one way to stay safe: keeping one's eyes on Jesus and not the craterous path flanked by the shadowy threat of the abyss. This is nothing new or unnatural; in fact

---

13 Adapted from Dietrich Bonhoeffer, *The Cost of Discipleship*, (New York, NY: Touchstone, 1959) p.190.

you've seen this play out every day of your life when you drive to work, school, or church. When driving, you don't look at your feet or hands or even at the road at the end of your hood (and certainly not the rearview mirror). No, you look down the road at where you want to go. If you looked at your feet, you would end up in a ditch or wrapped around a pole.

The same is true when following Christ on the path. At times it feels more like a tightrope than a trail. And like a tightrope, if you look at your feet, you're inevitably going to waiver.

Peter enacted this literally for us when he stepped out to meet his Lord on the Sea of Galilee.

But while the narrow road might be difficult and precarious, it is also by its very nature intimate. While on the world's wide road we might be able to isolate ourselves and spurn community, the narrow road inevitably forces those following it into community, into relationship not only with Christ but other believers.

The False Path of Fear/Dante's The Gates of Dis/Fear-Based Religion

As the pride of self-righteousness and religion in the end turn out to be an enemy of a humility-based faith, so too is fear. Fear, which has been used at times in some Christian communities as the primary motivator for the behavior of the community and the conversion of non-believers, is likewise an enemy of the Gospel. As we are told that "perfect love drives out fear" (1 John 4:18) and thus, a gospel based in love cannot simultaneously be based in fear.

Dante's *Inferno* contains a passage that illustrates this false (infernal) motivator beautifully. As Dante journeys with his spirit guide, Virgil, deeper and deeper into Hell, he comes upon a place that literally stops both of them in their tracks: the Gates of Dis. Atop the Gates of Dis stand the terrifying host of Hell, the Furies, screaming out threats, adorned with serpentine hair. The hideous creatures tell Dante and Virgil that they cannot pass through the daunting gates, warning that Medusa herself is coming to turn them into stone.

The threat does it trick, even terrifying the so far unshakable guide, Virgil. But just as Dante starts to believe that he will not be able to complete the journey which God has appointed him to travel, a Messenger from Heaven comes, says a few words, waves a wand, and the gates fly open. When Dante and Virgil finally pass through the gates, they find that all of the threats of Hell were empty. They find suffering souls in graves, but nothing that could stand against God's mercy.

The point is that fear, the Gates of Hell, as the foundation of faith is another false path. We are promised that the Gates of Hell cannot prevail against the Church (Matthew 16:18). As a body of believers, we should not be in the business of rebuilding the very gates Christ's work on the Cross and miracle in the Tomb have rendered powerless. The true gate that we should be focused on looks nothing like Dante's Gates of Dis. The true gate to life is characterized by humility, and sacrifice, and a love so profound that the world does not understand it. The true path to life must be walked in love, and takes us through the empty tomb.

The Journey through the Tomb

John Bickley, the coauthor of this book, conveyed to me a story about his time in Israel where his guide took them to, what many believe could have been, the Empty Tomb of Jesus. After an explanation about the historical

The gateway

to life

looks like

death.

context of the tomb—and the disclaimer that this very well might not be the true tomb of Christ—the guide invited the forty-odd tourists to enter the tomb when they saw fit.

The moments to follow were surprising to John and many of his fellow sojourners alike. Rather than a stampede toward the open door of the tomb, everyone fell silent. For a while, no one, not one person, moved.

The travelers had been invited to enter, but they would not... or could not. Eventually without prompting, tourist after tourist peeled off from the group, most moving away from the tomb rather than toward it.

Many sat down, as if overcome by the weight of the moment. Most, including John, wept at the overwhelming reality of what lay before them: The profundity of the tomb's emptiness. The difficult grace of the open invitation...

The gateway to life looks like death.

It is this reality that is perhaps the greatest reason why Jesus said in Matthew 7,

> "The highway to hell is broad, and its gate is wide for the many who choose that way. But the gateway to life is very narrow and the road is difficult, and only a few ever find it." (Matt 7:13-14, NLT)

The Gates of Heaven are hard to find because they do not look like gates at all. No gilded entrance with trumpets blaring. No fanfare, glitz, and glamour. Instead, a lowly, quiet, haunting tomb. But an empty tomb-and a tomb whose stone has been rolled away. The gateway to life looks like death.

The Power of the Empty Tomb

Many Christian apologists have pointed to the miraculous transformation that the disciples experienced upon Christ's resurrection as perhaps the most convincing historical evidence of Christ's resurrection. Peter goes from a posture of self-defense and cowardice in his three-time denial of Christ prior to the Resurrection, to an immovable rock of faith who lives and leads boldly, in the end facing—like almost every other disciple—a brutal death for his beliefs. The stories of the disciples' martyrdom are more than testaments to the Church of the power of unwavering faith, they are proof of the Resurrection and the power it has to transform each of us from selfish and fearful creatures into self-sacrificing and fearless messengers of God's great invitation to restored relationship.

The Watery Grave

Baptism is an important sacrament of the church in two distinct ways: the proclamation of a new disciple and the church receiving that new disciple into the body of Christ. The act of baptism also serves as a reminder of Christ's work on the Cross and the victory of the Empty Tomb.

In baptism, the believer is immersed under the water as an outward symbolic act that conveys the idea of dying to one's previous life before a restored relationship with God. The immersion is thus a symbolic following of Christ's lead, dying in obedience to God's will. In the same way, the emergence of the believer from the water parallels Christ rising from the tomb, enacting His victory over the wages of sin, death. In baptism, the believer symbolically follows the steps of Christ as he emerges from the tomb into a new life of restored relationship with God and the church.

The God of Beginnings

The Empty Tomb reminds us that often what we think are dead ends in our lives, in God's economy, can be new beginnings.

The idea that "He makes all things new" is perhaps best embodied in the symbol of the Empty Tomb: a serendipitous God reveals to the world His unquenchable love for His creation. A love which sees what may appear to finite eyes as lost causes, irredeemable failures, hopeless death spirals, inevitable losses, can prove to be the beginning of something we could never have seen coming - a restored relationship with God and people.

People who meet me today have a hard time envisioning the completely broken twenty-four year old Mark who was seriously considering ending his life. I tell the whole story in my first book, *Immersion: Live the Life God Envisioned for You*, but the important part of my story is that I needed not to take my own life, but to die to myself and live under the power, forgiveness, and leadership of the resurrected Jesus.

For me, the gateway to life had to be the death of my pride, arrogance, and control. It took God literally turning me around, blocking what I had come to believe was my destiny—a despair-filled drive off a tall cliff—and leading me instead to the beginning of hope, to a stone rolled away. And what is even more awe-inspiring is that in His infinite love, God performs this miracle every day, sometimes obviously, and oftentimes subtly.

The Living Christ

Perhaps in its most crucial state, the Empty Tomb serves to remind us that the center of the Christian faith is a living God. Without Christ's resurrection, Christianity would be a dead religion of worshippers kneeling before a sealed tomb. In other words, without the resurrection, the Christian faith would be like every other religion: a religion whose founder made profound proclamations, mentored followers, started a movement, died, and stayed dead.[14]

On account of the resurrection, Christianity is a living faith centered on a living Savior who has rolled away the stone that was blocking the path to an eternal life in relationship with Him.

---

[14] "The most startling characteristic of the first Christian preaching is its emphasis on the Resurrection. The first preachers were sure that Christ had risen, and sure, in consequence, that believers would in due course rise also. This set them off from all the other teachers of the ancient world. There are resurrections elsewhere, but none of them is like that of Christ. They are mostly mythological tales connected with the change of the season and the annual miracle of spring. The Gospels tell of an individual who truly died, but overcame death by rising again. And if it is true that Christ's resurrection bears no resemblance to anything in Paganism, it is also true that the attitude of believers to their own resurrection, the corollary of their Lord's, is radically different from anything in the heathen world. Nothing is more characteristic of even the best thought of the day than its hopelessness in the face of death. Clearly the Resurrection is of the very first importance for the Christian faith.
The Christian idea of resurrection is to be distinguished from both Greek and Jewish ideas. The Greeks thought of the body as a hindrance to true life and they looked for the time when the soul would be free from its shackles. They conceived of life after death in terms of the immortality of the soul, but they firmly rejected all ideas of resurrection (cf. The mockery of Paul's preaching in Acts 17:32). The Jews were firmly persuaded of the values of the body, and thought these would not be lost. They thus looked for the body to be raised. But they thought it would be exactly the same body (Apocalypse of Baruch 1:2). The Christians thought of the body as being raised, but also transformed so as to be a suitable vehicle for the very different life of the age to come (1 Cor. 15:42ff.). The Christian idea is thus distinctive." (Wood, D. R. W., & Marshall, I. H. (1996). New Bible Dictionary (3rd ed.) (1010). Leicester, England; Downers Grove, IL: Intervarsity Press.)

GOING
DEEPER

BREAKING GROUND

What was a time in your life when you were caught by surprise by something you had actually been told beforehand would happen?

THE DIG

How important to the Christian faith is Jesus' resurrection from the dead?

What impact does the Empty Tomb have on the Cross and the Life of Christ? (1 Corinthians 15:12-20)

How did Jesus' resurrection impact his followers? How did they act before His resurrection and after?

In what ways are our reactions to His resurrection either similar or different to theirs?

Why is the Christian Church more focused on Christ's death than His resurrection?

Why is the Empty Tomb difficult or even a hindrance to people approaching Christianity? (p. 69)

How does the Empty Tomb relate to the Christian paradox of death leading to life?

Why do you have to die to yourself in order to experience life in Christ?

Why is it hard for people to walk the causeway between legalism and hedonism (thought that pleasure is the only intrinsic good)?

How do you keep on the straight and narrow?

GETTING OUT OF THE HOLE

What is one area in your life in which you still need to die to yourself and live in Christ?

How will you leave behind the past and let God make things new?

Search the Scriptures for what it means to have the mind of Christ and ask God to give you wisdom. Exercise your faith by responding to God's promises and sharing those truths with others.

SUPPORTING RESOURCES

Here are a few suggestions for continued study:

Strobel, Lee. *The Case for the Resurrection*. Grand Rapids, MI: Zondervan, 2010.

Habermas, Gary and Licona, Michael. *The Case for the Resurrection of Jesus*. Grand Rapids, MI: Kregel, 2004.

SYMBOL FIVE:
THE FISH

THE CHURCH

> "Jesus's resurrection is the beginning of God's new project, not to snatch people away from earth to heaven, but to colonize earth with the life of heaven."
> - N.T. Wright, Surprised by Hope: Rethinking Heaven, the Resurrection, and the Mission of the Church

Symbol Explanation: the Fish

The church has used the Fish, or ΙΧΘΥΣ (Greek for "fish"), as a symbol for its faith from the first centuries of its existence, when persecution of Christians by the Roman Empire was rampant.

Tradition has it that the two simple arcs of the fish could be subtly drawn with the foot in the dirt to identify fellow believers. Christians also sometimes carved or painted the symbol on important sites to mark meeting places.

The reasons for choosing the fish as a symbol for Christianity are numerous. One is word game: the Greek word *Ichthys* (ΙΧΘΥΣ, "fish") was an acrostic for "Jesus Christ God's Son Savior" (*Iesous Christos Theou Yios Soter*).

Biblical connections are obviously important as well. As Christ declared to Peter and Andrew when he first called him,

> "Follow me, and I will make you fishers of men."
> (Matt 4:19, ESV)

Christ's miraculous multiplication of the two fish and five loaves is another clear reference. A less overt one, as pointed out by Christianity Today's Elisha Coffman, is the parallel created between converts and fish through baptismal immersion in water.[14]

Jesus also specifically references the most famous fish in the Old Testament when he stated prophetically that his sign would be the Sign of Jonah (Matt 12:39).

The Commission
The Christian Church exists because of the resurrected Christ; it was not until Jesus' resurrection that the disciples were commissioned. It was the risen Christ, who gave the Great Commission to His disciples:

"I have been given all authority in heaven and on earth. Therefore, go and make disciples of all the nations, baptizing them in the name of the Father and the Son and the Holy Spirit. Teach these new disciples to obey all the commands I have given you. And be sure of this: I am with you always, even to the end of the age." (Mt 28:18–20)

Jesus' declaration that He has complete authority in heaven and earth is a daily challenge to any person who dares to call himself or herself a follower of Christ. Perhaps this is why Jesus said in Luke 9,

---

[14] "The Fish has plenty of other theological overtones as well, for Christ fed the 5,000 with 2 fishes and 5 loaves (a meal recapitulated in Christian love-feasts) and called his disciples "fishers of men." water baptism, practiced by immersion in the early church, created a parallel between fish and converts. Second-century theologian Tertullian put it this way: 'We, little fishes, after the image of our *Ichthys*, Jesus Christ, are born in the water.'" (Elisha Coffman, *Christianity Today*, "What is the Origin of the Christian Fish Symbol?" Http://www.christianitytoday.com/ch/asktheexpert/oct26.html)

> "If any of you wants to be my follower, you must turn
> from your selfish ways, take up your cross daily, and
> follow me." (Luke 9:23, NLT)

Following Jesus' teachings and life example are the default and final word in all life decisions, reinforced by the conscious decision to die to yourself each and every day and submit to the complete authority of the risen Lord.

Interestingly enough, although following Christ is a personal decision, it is not an individual effort, but rather a *peloton* of faith.[15]

I am a big fan of competitive cycling and racing; in fact, I also coach a junior cycling team which is sponsored by our church's coffee bar (www.redeyevelo.com). I try to explain to the kids that cyclists in a peloton, or group, save energy by riding close behind other cyclists. This is known as drafting. The reduction in energy is dramatic: in the middle of a peloton a cyclist can save as much as 30% of his/her energy compared to riding alone. This doesn't even take into account the encouragement to go faster and longer than if you were cycling on your own.

Perhaps like Christianity, this reduction in effort and increased encouragement when cycling in a group is why the writer of Hebrews wrote,

> "And let us not neglect our meeting together, as some
> people do, but encourage one another, especially now
> that the day of his return is drawing near."
> (Hebrews 10:25, NLT)

---

[15] A peloton (from French, meaning "little ball or platoon") in cycling refers to the main group of riders in a road bicycle race.

I'm going to go out on a limb here, but I am very skeptical of a "just me and Jesus" faith. While I'll apprehensively concede someone can conceivably follow Christ on his/her own, I would also push back that the Christian faith at its essence is having a right relationship with God and people; this is the Gospel as modeled by Jesus.

Jesus so loved the world, that He left perfect community with the Father and Holy Spirit to live in community with people and to make a way for them to experience an abundant life which is an overflowing blessing to others. Self-amputation from the Body of Christ, the Church, is rejecting the blessing and subjecting oneself to the very core of the curse; the isolation and separation from which Jesus came to save us.[16]

The Church, as in cycling, helps make positive progress a lot easier when the peloton, or Body of Christ, is working together toward a common purpose.

"Unattached"

When I first started racing, I was not on a team. If you took the time to look at my unimpressive cycling career, you would see that USA Cycling listed my team affiliation as "Unattached."

Unattached does not mean I did not race or that I wasn't doing my best to win. It simply meant I was not on a team. Interestingly enough, if you look at the results, you will notice that most of the people at the top of the list are on a team, and as the logic would follow, most of the people on the bottom of

---

[16] For further reading on the essence of Christian community, see Stanley Grenz, *Created for Community* (Wheaton, IL: Victor Books, 1996), 205-250. See also Gilbert Bilezikian and John Ortberg, *Community 101: Reclaiming the Local Church as Community of Oneness* (Grand Rapids, MI: Zondervan, 1997).

the list are "unattached." This is not to say you can't win if you are unattached, it is just a lot harder to achieve your potential as a cyclist.

The same is true with being connected with a local body of believers. A lot of pastors call people who don't go to church "Unchurched." I am not a fan of this terminology for two reasons. First, it implies that the goal is to get someone "churched," which is not our God-given mission. Second, it could easily be interpreted as having something to do with a person's status in God's eyes. Besides, what does "churched" mean exactly? Actively participating in church—or "religious indoctrination"?

I prefer the term "unattached" for Christians who are not part of a local body. Like an unattached cyclist, they feel confident they can go it alone, and they don't yet understand the benefits of being a part of a peloton of faith.

The Banquet v. the Resort Spa

The "unattached" conception of one's faith is one of the dangerous byproducts of the popular Western Gospel presentation of Heaven as being a personal, resort/spa, paradise destination. There is no evident need or purpose for the Church in this narrow presentation of the Gospel.

The biblical reality is that we are invited to participate in a banquet with our friends and family—a banquet thrown for the redeemed by God the Father.

Perhaps no other parable of Christ communicates God's invitation to be in community with Him and His creation better than in Luke 14.

Jesus responds to a man asking about the Kingdom of God by telling a story about a banquet. He uses the parable to illustrate the mission of His followers, His Church, and His desire to be in relationship with His creation.

The parable begins with an invitation:

> "A man prepared a great feast and sent out many invitations. When the banquet was ready, he sent his servant to tell the guests, 'Come, the banquet is ready.'"
> (Luke 14:16b-17, NLT)

As is the case in all of his parables, Jesus establishes a prominent metaphor: the "great feast," or banquet, is a metaphor of communion with God, unfettered love, and connection with Jesus.

Notice what God does. He sends out many invitations, not

Be Ready

An often overlooked element here is that the guests were not told to come until the banquet was ready. Think about this in your own context; if you are invited somewhere, you expect that the host is prepared to receive you at the given time. In fact, it would be irresponsible and rude to invite people to a party you are not prepared to give. This is a mistake a lot of churches make. They eagerly invite people to the church without giving any thought to the menu, activities, or logistics of how they are going to serve their guests when they arrive.

demands, threats, or scare tactics—invitations. This invitational approach is critical to the comprehension of the parable.

Notice that when the banquet was ready, he sent his servants. The host did not go himself. The servants went as the ambassadors or personifications of the banquet invitation. When you personify the characteristics of God you are, perhaps more than anything else, living a life of invitation.

> "But they all began making excuses. One said, 'I have just bought a field and must inspect it. Please excuse me.' Another said, 'I have just bought five pairs of oxen, and I want to try them out. Please excuse me.' Another said, 'I now have a wife, so I can't come.'"
> (Luke 14:18-20, NLT)

This portion of the parable carries a punch. It reveals the reality of rejection and the mundane reasons for refusing to attend the banquet. It also illustrates another profound point, one laced with hope: Just because you choose not to come doesn't mean you weren't invited.

> "The servant returned and told his master what they had said. His master was furious and said, 'Go quickly into the streets and alleys of the town and invite the poor, the crippled, the blind, and the lame.' After the servant had done this, he reported, 'There is still room for more.' So his master said, 'Go out into the country lanes and behind the hedges and urge anyone you find to come, so that the house will be full. For none of those I first invited will get even the smallest taste of my banquet.' " (Luke 14:21-24, NLT)

This echoes God's metanarrative, the overarching story of salvation. In an unanticipated demonstration of grace, God opens up the invitation to those who never saw it coming.[17]

Being the Invitation

Perhaps the most monumental discovery for a follower of Christ is the realization that we are the invitation (2 Cor. 5:18-20). But we must make sure we are inviting people to the right occasion. Are we out there giving a sales pitch for a beautiful destination, or are we inviting others into a relationship?

Recently, my friend and fellow Pastor Billy Robertson posted an insightful discussion of what true invitation looks like, differentiating the relational Gospel from the fabled sales pitch of the destination gospel. Here's the full post:

> *The destination gospel has to be presented with a "sales pitch" many times in order to get people to "buy." Let's look at some "sales pitches" explaining salvation: "Believe in Jesus, or you're going to Hell." Or "Heaven is going to be so awesome; it has streets of gold, columns of pearl, etc., etc., etc. accept Jesus, today." or "Heaven is going to be a great party, with no more pain, no suffering, no sorrow and to get there all you have to do is believe in Jesus."*

> *Those statements may have some truth to them, but we are missing the forest for trees. The destination gospel*

---

[17] For more on this parable see: David Wenham, The Parables of Jesus (Downers Grove, IL: InterVarsity Press, 1989), 133-138; Brad Young, The Parables: Jewish Interpretation and Christian Tradition (Peabody, MA: Hendrickson Publishers, 1998), 171-186; Robert Farrar Capon, Kingdom, Grace, Judgment: Paradox, Outrage, and Vindication in the Parables of Jesus (Grand Rapids, MI: Eerdmans Publishing Co., 2002), 272-301.

commands more respect and adoration for the destination than the One Who created the destination.

The destination pales in comparison to the main Character. The destination is only Glory because the Glorious One resides there! The Yankees have never said come to Yankee Stadium, because the stadium is awesome. They said come here to see the Babe, or Mickey, or Lou, or Joe. We didn't go to Graceland to see the jungle room, we went to see the king, but that king is no longer there.

The King in the Kingdom, His companionship, and our restored friends and family is what makes the destination, Heaven, not the angels, not the streets, not the mansions, but the Creator. (Billy Robertson)

The Body of Christ: Illuminating

The mission of the Body of Christ is to continue the work of Jesus in the world until His return and fulfillment of the promise made to the Israelites. (John 17, in my opinion, is one of the best synopses of Jesus' ministry. A great exercise is to go through John 17 and highlight all the "I did" statements Jesus makes.)

More directly, Jesus commissions his followers in Matthew 28:19-20 in what many scholars call, "The Great Commission." In The Great Commission, Jesus instructs His followers to do three things:

- Make disciples/followers
- Baptize the disciples/followers
- Teach the disciples/followers

As the body of Christ, our calling is to be the personification of God's character and the guiding fire in this world needing to be reconciled with Him and others.

"...illuminate, not burn."
So what does it look like to be the personification of God's character? Seems like a rather tall order.

A beautiful and insightful young lady who goes to our church in Tallahassee, Rikki, wrote in one of our church's devotionals that "Our fire should illuminate, not burn." I would like to attempt to add an extra point to Rikki's profound statement.

Before electricity, batteries, and centralized heating and air-conditioning, fires were not only nice, they were essential for human existence. They gave heat, light, safety, and comfort. A fire communicated in many ways that the home was awake and ready for guests. I'm sure you have heard the saying, "We'll keep the home fire lit." The meaning is that they are ready, even eager, to receive the other as their guest.

Fire is important to someone's well-being, but it is also a sign of invitation. And a life of invitation is the personification of God.

Many people feel that our Christ-given mission to invite people into the Gospel story is somehow an annoyance or negative. But an invitation from a friend is almost never received negatively. Have you ever been upset because someone you like invited you to something? Of course not. In reality, the times you have been upset is because you were not invited to something.

The truth is, a personal invitation—even if a person is not interested in the event—communicates love, a desire for a deeper relationship, and value to the invitee. God is a God of invitation, and when we personify invitation, God is making His appeal through us.

The Joyful Fire

So where does this inner illumination come from? Joy.

Christ is the path, not only to a joy that transcends all circumstances, but to an overflowing joy that goes beyond our own life capacity and blesses others. This is our invitation.

This overflowing joy cannot be conjured up through self-realized holiness or self-actualization, but only by following His spiritual path. This is why Jesus said,

"Remain in my love. When you obey my commandments, you remain in my love, just as I obey my Father's commandments and remain in his love. I have told you these things so that you will be filled with my joy. Yes, your joy will overflow! (John 15:9–11, NLT)

The Spirit of God

The imperfect Church has been given the perfect mission to be the avatar of Christ, commissioned to prepare God's creation for the Kingdom of God to come and complete the Story of Israel. The Church, in its ideal state, is supposed to be the physical manifestation of the person and teaching of Jesus

Christ. It can only be so through Him; by being filled with the joy of His love.

The Church as the embodiment of God on earth is why the Apostle Paul refers to the Church as the Body of Christ, and it is this body (the Church) that has been commissioned to carry out His work.

The exciting thing is that Christ sent the same power that raised Him from the dead to indwell in His followers.[18] Jesus gave us the Holy Spirit to not only carry on His work, but to take it to the next level. It is hard to believe, but Jesus told His followers in John 14:12,

> "I tell you the truth, anyone who believes in me will do the same works I have done, and even greater works, because I am going to be with the Father."
> (John 14:12, NLT)

I know this seems like a bold proclamation, but it is true. Think about it (beyond the unrepeatable final work of the cross), the Body of Christ has done greater works than Jesus. Jesus healed perhaps hundreds of people, where His Church has healed perhaps millions of people. Where Jesus fed thousands of people, His Church has fed millions. Where Jesus discipled hundreds of people, His Church has discipled billions of people. And where Jesus illuminated a few hundred square miles of the Middle East, His Church has illuminated just about the entire world.

---

[18] Romans 8:11 "The Spirit of God, who raised Jesus from the dead, lives in you. And just as God raised Christ Jesus from the dead, he will give life to your mortal bodies by this same Spirit living within you."

These miracles, which are "greater" than even what Jesus performed, are not just what is happening out there, but it is what is happening in you. For example, at 44 years old I am a blessed man. God has blessed me with a beautiful and godly wife, two wonderful children, a great family, and an awesome church. He has surrounded me with people who care about me and cause my life to overflow with love.

When friends and family started asking me what I would like for my birthday last year, I really could not come up with anything. Then the day before my birthday during my prayer time, I thought about a six year old boy who lives in Haiti named Jovens.

Jovens doesn't smile.

The reason Jovens doesn't smile is because he was born with a malformed leg. It is about half the size of his working leg with a small backward and useless foot on the end. But the malformed leg is not really why Jovens does not smile - it is because he has been discarded by his community as worthless. In the Spring of last year, my dear friend Michael, using his mad physical therapy skills fitted him for some crutches. With his mother watching and crying, Jovens took his first steps but Jovens still did not smile.

Fast forward to last Fall, a week before my birthday. Michael got back from another trip to Haiti and told me God had put it on his heart to find a way to get Jovens the surgery he needed, which would allow him to be fitted for a prosthetic leg. Then Jovens would have a chance in life. In my prayer time the day before my birthday, the Holy Spirit put in my mind's eye the image of Jovens smiling. I don't know your theology, but to me that is a God given vision and an opportunity to be the tangible hand of Christ.

But how? I'm a doctor, but as my kids like to remind me, I'm not the kind of doctor who helps people. I don't have the money to pay for this kind of operation, and I wouldn't even know how to begin to set it up. But the Holy Spirit kept prompting me to just trust and simply post my birthday wish on Facebook.

Honestly, I have never wanted anything so badly for my birthday, so with some reluctance because of pride, I made a simple Facebook post expressing my birthday wish.

When I woke up the next morning, with tears in my eyes I stared reading messages from my fellow Facebookers. In less than 24 hours, we had not only raised the money for Jovens surgery but also the money for the initial travel for him and his mother to Port au Prince, Haiti. If that weren't amazing enough, a Canadian surgeon agreed to perform the surgery and a prosthetics doctor whom I had never met from a different part of the country contacted me wanting to be part of Jovens' miracle.

Was Jesus using hyperbole when He said, "I tell you the truth, anyone who believes in me will do the same works I have done, and even greater works, because I am going to be with the Father" (John 14:12, NLT)? I don't think so.

Yes, Jesus was telling the truth and I believe there is nothing more beautiful (and powerful) than when the Bride of Christ allows the Holy Spirit to empower their lives so that the Church can be the full expression of God's love in this lost and hurting world.[19]

The Body of Christ has been commissioned to go and make disciples, baptize them, and teach them how to follow Jesus. We have been invited to be the light of the world, a messenger of the greatest love story ever told. As inconceivable as it may seem, it is your time and your calling to be the tangible hand of Christ in your home, work, community, and world. There is no Plan B. You are it. But you are not alone; in fact, the very power that raised Jesus from the dead lives in you, and that is why the Gates of Hell will not stand.[20]

---

[19] 1 John 4:12 "No one has ever seen God. But if we love each other, God lives in us, and his love is brought to full expression in us."

[20] Romans 8:11 (NLT) "The Spirit of God, who raised Jesus from the dead, lives in you. And just as God raised Christ Jesus from the dead, He will give life to your mortal bodies by this same spirit living within you."

GOING
DEEPER

BREAKING GROUND

What was the best team of which you were ever a part?

Why was this team so good?

What did the team accomplish?

THE DIG

Read Matthew 28:18-20.

What are the three directives Jesus gives His disciples?

1.

2.

3.

How is making disciples different than making converts?

What does being a disciple of Jesus involve?

Why do you think baptism is connected to discipleship?

Why is baptism important to Jesus?

What is the connection between baptism and discipleship?

If the third directive is to teach, then what can be learned about effective teaching from your favorite teacher?

Why is the church important in a follower of Christ's life?

Read Hebrews 10:25.

Why is meeting together important for a Christian?

Why does Jesus use banquets and weddings as imagery for both a healthy church and heaven?

What simile would you use to describe your church? "My church is like…"

Read Romans 8:11 & John 14:12.
How has the Holy Spirit empowered the Church to do even greater works than Jesus?

Read 1 John 4:12.
How has your church facilitated you to be the full expression of God's love?

GETTING OUT OF THE HOLE
Discuss ways your group can be the full expression of God's love in your community?

SUPPORTING RESOURCES
Here are a few suggestions for continued study:

Rainer, Thom. *I Am a Church Member.* Nashville, TN: B & H Publishing, 2013.

Chester, Tim and Timmis, Steve. *Total Church*. Wheaton, IL: Crossway Books, 2008.

SYMBOL SIX:
INFINITE LOVE

AN UNBUFFERED RELATIONSHIP WITH GOD

> "Though we are incomplete, God loves us completely.
> Though we are imperfect, He loves us perfectly.
> Though we may feel lost and without compass, God's
> love encompasses us completely." - Dieter F. Uchtdorf

Symbol Explanation of Infinite Love

The symbol for Infinite Love is a new addition to iconography. It is formed by superimposing the pop-culture icon for Heart over the ancient and ubiquitous symbol for Infinity. This symbol is obviously not a historical Christian symbol, but it does encapsulate, in a readily recognizable way, the idea of the endless love God offers His creation. The love story of the Gospel has shown us that God has an unquenchable desire to be in relationship with His creation and has gone through extraordinary measures to make restoration a reality.

The Only Way?

I am asked the following question all the time, "Is Jesus the only way to heaven?" My standard answer is, "If you could get there any other way, you would not want to be there." Which is usually followed by, "Why?" Because Heaven is Heaven not because of the Pearly Gates or streets of gold, but because of the unfettered presence of Jesus.

The Apostle John proclaimed, "Look, God's home is now among his people! He will live with them, and they will be his people. God himself will be with them" (Rev 21:3, NLT). This is to say, what makes Heaven Heaven is God among His people. Without God it cannot be Heaven and since Heaven is not a destination, a person cannot be forced into it. What makes Heaven, well, Heaven is God, and Jesus is God.[21]

I am sure you have had someone try to force a relationship on you in the past; it is a vile and horrific experience—the antithesis of the kind of love God offers his sons and daughters.

It is not a pleasant experience. In fact, our society has a word for a person who tries to force himself into your life: a stalker. A stalker is at least irritating, and at worst frightening. Jesus is not a stalker.

In Revelation 3, Jesus declares, "Look! I stand at the door and knock. If you hear my voice and open the door, I will come in, and we will share a meal together as friends" (Rev 3:20, NLT). Here the truth is revealed about the nature of Christ: He desires to be in relationship with you. He'll even come to you in order to make that relationship possible, but it is you who must welcome Him in.

The unfettered presence of Jesus in His full majesty and deity can only be paradise if someone has a longing to experience Infinite Love. A.W. Tozer, said, "I can safely say, on the authority

---

[21] Colossians 1:15-20 Christ is the visible image of the invisible God. He existed before anything was created and is supreme over all creation, for through him God created everything in the heavenly realms and on earth. He made the things we can see and the things we can't see—such as thrones, kingdoms, rulers, and authorities in the unseen world. Everything was created through him and for him. He existed before anything else, and he holds all creation together. Christ is also the head of the church, which is his body. He is the beginning, supreme over all who rise from the dead. So he is first in everything. For God in all his fullness was pleased to live in Christ, and through him God reconciled everything to himself. He made peace with everything in heaven and on earth by means of Christ's blood on the cross.

of all that is revealed in the Word of God, that any man or woman on this earth who is bored and turned off by worship is not ready for heaven."

Why did Tozer say that? Because heaven is the unfettered presence of Jesus. Imagine the closest you have ever felt God in a worship gathering; that is only a hazy glimpse of the future clarity of the Son.

John Piper put it this way: "The critical question for our generation—and for every generation—is this: If you could have heaven, with no sickness, and with all the friends you ever had on earth, and all the food you ever liked, and all the leisure activities you ever enjoyed, and all the natural beauties you ever saw, all the physical pleasures you ever tasted, and no human conflict or any natural disasters, could you be satisfied with heaven, if Christ were not there?"[22]

I love this question, because your answer will reveal your understanding of Heaven.

I can't tell you how many times I've heard someone explain Heaven as some sort of cosmic Disneyland. Many times, the presenter fails to even mention the presence of Jesus. The reality is when you disconnect Jesus from Heaven, you end up with dismal theology. If you don't like Jesus, you don't want to go to Heaven; Heaven is Heaven because of Jesus' unfettered presence. Heaven without Jesus would be Hell.

---

[22] John Piper, *God Is the Gospel: Meditations on God's Love as the Gift of Himself* (Wheaton, IL: Crossway Books, 2005), 15.

This is all said without a hint of condemnation for those who have an unbiblical understanding of Heaven. This misaligned perspective lies at the feet of advocates of the Destination Gospel, those who use the "feature/benefit" sales pitch. We've all heard ad nauseum: "If you say this prayer, you'll get a ticket to paradise. But if you don't...."

Again, the Destination Gospel removes the person of Christ from the Gospel and it also removes the passion and love the Creator has for His creation. An earthly equivalent would be to build a home for your family, installing every detail with your spouse and kids in mind: sparkling pool, stainless steel appliances, and spa-like master bathroom. On the big move in day, you text a Google map to your family of the house address and permanently leave town.

What would be their response? Did your family want a house or did they want to live in a beautiful home with you? If your family is even just semi-functioning in a healthy manner, the answer is unequivocally a home with you.

The Godly Shadow

"For these rules are only shadows of the reality yet to come. And Christ himself is that reality." (Col 2:17, NLT)

Sure, most of us have experienced a godly shadow of Infinite Love in our lives. For some, a godly shadow of love may have been cast by a mother standing in the light of the LORD while others may have been covered by the warm shadow of a lifelong friend or spouse. As wonderful and seemingly complete as this love is, it is only a shadow of the reality to come. Christ himself is that reality.

Imagine, if you will, an Infinite Love that is as different from the purest love we have known in this life as the reflection of the sun on the water is from the sun itself. Or to use the shadow metaphor: as different as a two-dimensional shadow of a person is from the three-dimensional, flesh and blood person casting that shadow.

This love would be a perfect and complete love - a love that would envelop you in complete acceptance and commitment. For the first time in your life, you will experience an Infinite Love that completely knows you and—despite that intimate knowledge of all your imperfections—affirms and envelops you in a perfect, endless love.

You are invited into this perfect relationship because God desires to be in an unfettered relationship with you. This is the great expectation that the writer of Hebrews wrote about in chapter 10:

"And so, dear brothers and sisters, we can boldly enter heaven's Most Holy Place because of the blood of Jesus." (Heb. 10:19, NLT)

Imagine being able to walk boldly into Heaven's Most Holy Place because of the unending love of Jesus. One of my favorite worship songs that captures the heart of Hebrews 10:19 is "God Will Lift up your Head," a 17th-century German hymn, written by Paul Gerhardt (and recently made famous by Jars of Clay in 2005).

This song describes the tension that a subject would have felt approaching a king in antiquity. In antiquity, when subjects would approach the throne, they would be required to approach with their heads lowered in an external act of submission and reverence to the power and majesty of the king. The subjects would keep their heads down until the king decided to accept or reject their presence. If accepted, the king would reach down and lift up the heads of the subjects, signaling they were now the guests of the king.

The imagery of Hebrews 10:19 portrays a very different relationship between the King and His subjects. Because Jesus paid the price for His creation's rebellion against perfect love, we do not enter as subjects, but as family. We boldly enter as princesses and princes of the King Most High. This is why the Apostle Paul said in Romans 8, "So you have not received a spirit that makes you fearful slaves. Instead, you received God's Spirit when he adopted you as his own children. Now we call him, 'Abba, Father'" (Rom 8:15, NLT).

What Paul is speaking about here is the restoration of the ideal state. In this ideal state, Christ's followers will experience an unfettered and unbuffered relationship with their Creator, this is Heaven. Paul's use of the word Abba for God, conveys intimacy, as it is a word used between young children and their loving father. The image of Heaven Paul is painting is not intrusive— one ruled by the watchful eye of an impatient judge— but one immersed in the loving and protective embrace of the Father, Daddy.

This ideal state, especially when labeled as Heaven, is often a point of contention with many non-believers. I was once invited to speak on a panel alongside a man who claimed to be an atheist. He claimed that Christianity is a religion of fear because it says that if you are bad, you get thrown into a pit with scary monsters, and if you are good, you get to live on a fluffy cloud.

Since he said this in his closing thought and I had already spoken, I asked him afterwards if I could paint a different picture of Heaven and Hell for him. Predictably, he didn't want to hear it. But if he had lent me his ear, this is the heavenly portrait I hoped to convey:

The Ideal State

"When the cool evening breezes were blowing, the man and his wife heard the LORD God walking about in the garden." (Gen 3:8a, NLT)

Right before "the curse" was ushered in by humanity's rebellion, a glimpse of the ideal state between God and His creation was revealed in Genesis 3:8. Here we are given a beautiful picture of how God envisions a right relationship between Himself and His creation. Notice what time of day God came to meet with who we now know as Adam and Eve: "When the cool evening breezes were blowing...." Not when their betrayal happened; not in the heat of the day. No, He came when it was the most comfortable for them, when the "cool evening breezes were blowing." Then notice how He came not on a war horse of judgment, but walking about in the garden.

The ideal state of God and His creation is not of slave and master, or judge and accused, but a beautiful, healthy, and intimate relationship. This is the confident hope that is spoken about nineteen different times in the New Testament. A follower of Christ's anticipation comes from the confident hope of what God has reserved for him/her in heaven. (I'll refer to as the Ideal State 2.0 later in this chapter.)[23]

Current State

"I press on to reach the end of the race and receive the heavenly prize for which God, through Christ Jesus, is calling us." (Phil 3:14, NLT)

In my previous book, *Immersion: Live the Life God Envisioned for You*, I wrote about winning the heavenly prize Paul is speaking about as well as winning in our current state.

Winning is experiencing what God originally envisioned for His creation. In other words, winning is becoming what God created us to be: fully human. That might make some sense from a theological or semantical perspective, but what does that mean for us practically?

We were created to have an intimate relationship with our Creator. There have only been three people ever to walk this planet who have experienced being fully human: Adam, Eve, and Jesus. Being fully human is having an unfettered connection and interaction with God: The Ideal State.

Since the Garden, however, the current state of God's creation is disconnected and only a shadow of the abundant life God had envisioned for His creation.

---

[23] Colossians 1:5 Which come from your confident hope of what God has reserved for you in heaven. You have had this expectation ever since you first heard the truth of the Good News.

A relationship with God is just like, not unlike any other relationship in life. Sometimes, it's all we can do not to put our own wants and desires above the other person's needs. Similarly, the Ideal State with God is damaged when people choose their own selfish desires over God's desire to be intimate with them. This results in a relational rift with God leaving us with the empty feeling that something is missing in life.

Paul describes the current state as looking "through a glass, darkly" — experiencing life as if looking through a clouded window, ever separated from the true life that waits on the other side. However, you don't have to resign yourself to a clouded and shadowy existence. You are not hopelessly condemned to a separated buffered life.

The essence of the Gospel is that God loves you so much that from the onset of the severed relationship, He promised to make a way for restoration. That way was Jesus, who came to remove the buffer, break down the barrier between you and God, and to restore your full humanity.

This restoration was paid in full for you by the ultimate sacrifice of the separation of the Son from the Father. Clearly the opportunity to have a right relationship with God and His creation is not free, but more accurately the price has already been paid.

Our church's coffee bar, RedEye Coffee (www.RE3EYE. com), owns a repurposed school short bus that we serve complementary coffee out of at local events around our city. When we give people coffee they often comment how they can't believe it is free. I reply it is not free, but the price has already been paid. My hope with this little Gospel humor is that the sacred echoes of grace will resonate in the person's life.

The Good News of Jesus does not have a price you must pay because the price has already been paid. The sales pitch of "the free gift of salvation" has made many conclude that grace is cheap, but grace is far from cheap or free, it carried with it an exacting price that we will never fully understand this side of Heaven.

As passionate as Jesus is for you, He did not come as a brute to force you into a relationship with God; He came to show you how to live and give you the opportunity to move toward the relationship you were designed to experience. Those who choose to move into this relationship have the "confident hope" that they will someday experience what it means to be fully human.[24]

For now, Christians are like the Apostle Paul who said,

> "No, dear brothers and sisters, I have not achieved it, but I focus on this one thing: Forgetting the past and looking forward to what lies ahead, I press on to reach the end of the race and receive the heavenly prize for which God, through Christ Jesus, is calling us."
> (Phil 3:13, NLT)

What is the heavenly prize? Being "fully human" and experiencing unbuffered intimacy with God. Until that day, we

---

[24] Romans 12:12 "Rejoice in our confident hope. Be patient in trouble, and keep on praying."

are in a state of anticipation.

State of Anticipation

> "But we are citizens of heaven, where the Lord Jesus Christ lives. And we are eagerly waiting for him to return as our Savior." (Phil 3:20, NLT)

Although a follower of Christ's citizenship is secure, Christians are in a state of anticipation waiting for Jesus' return to complete the story of Israel and usher in a new and permanent ideal state characterized by a right relationship with God and His creation. The Apostle Paul concisely encapsulates this state of anticipation when he writes,

> "And we believers also groan, even though we have the Holy Spirit within us as a foretaste of future glory, for we long for our bodies to be released from sin and suffering. We, too, wait with eager hope for the day when God will give us our full rights as his adopted children, including the new bodies he has promised us." (Romans 8:23, NLT)

Existing in a state of anticipation can be exhilarating and frustrating at the same time. Like anticipating your first kiss, road trip vacation, or graduation, many times a person will miss the beauty of the journey by focusing on the destination. Brandon Sanderson poetically captures the tension people feel with future anticipation in his axiom: "Life before Death. Strength before Weakness. Journey before Destination."[25]

---

[25] Brandon Sanderson, *The Way of Kings* (New York, NY: Tor Books, 2011), 59.

Although, Sanderson is not talking about the Christian journey or Heaven, he does succinctly make the point for honoring the process and existing in the present day. As James writes, "Remember, it is sin to know what you ought to do and then not do it" (James 4:17, NLT). As I discussed in Symbol Five: The Fish, the Church's mission is to continue the work of Jesus in the world until He returns, fulfilling the promise made to the Israelites. So, if we could change the quote to serve as a Christian axiom, it may go, "Love before Intimacy. Surrender before Discipleship. Worship before Ideal."

Ideal State 2.0

"I saw no temple in the city, for the Lord God Almighty and the Lamb are its temple." (Rev 21:22, NLT)

In the end we are reminded by John in Revelation 21:22, that the ideal state is not the Garden of Eden, but the unfiltered presence of God—the result of which is the experience of Infinite Love.

This ideal state will be creation come full circle. We will no longer require a buffer, a mediator. In other words, though it might sound counterintuitive, we will no longer require the temple/church. As the ideal state of humanity in Eden began without the need of a temple/church, our redeemed ideal state will conclude without the need for a temple/church.

This is not to say the temple/church East of Eden is bad. Of course not. The temple/church stands as a marker for humanity, a proclamation of His love and desire for us to experience the perfectly woven tapestry of a holy (perfect) relationship. But it looks ahead to a time when we will no longer need it-a time when will live in the unmediated presence of God.

God's full presence will be complete, the likes of which we've only experienced but a hint, a shadow. This perfectly restored immersion into Infinite Love is the "great expectation" that Peter speaks about in his letter to the outlying churches of the Roman Empire.

"All praise to God, the Father of our Lord Jesus Christ. It is by his great mercy that we have been born again, because God raised Jesus Christ from the dead. Now we live with great expectation, and we have a priceless inheritance—an inheritance that is kept in heaven for you, pure and undefiled, beyond the reach of change and decay. And through your faith, God is protecting you by his power until you receive this salvation, which is ready to be revealed on the last day for all to see." (1 Peter 1:3–5, NLT)

The core hope of a follower of Christ is the great expectation that we will someday experience a fully restored and perfect relationship with our Creator in the manner God originally envisioned. Our lives here on earth are supposed to be lives characterized by "great expectation"--an excitement and anticipation about what is to come, which Peter calls a "priceless inheritance."

The Apostle Paul speaks about the anticipation of this holy and perfect loving relationship as a great mystery, clouded because of his own brokenness that obscures his ability to see love clearly.

"Now we see things imperfectly, like puzzling reflections in a mirror, but then we will see everything with perfect clarity. All that I know now is partial and incomplete, but then I will know everything completely, just as God now knows me completely. Three things will last forever—faith, hope, and love—and the greatest of these is love." (1 Corinthians 13:12–13, NLT)

The reality is that no one has experienced or even has the current capacity to understand a perfect and eternal love. People have experienced hints of what Paul discusses: exercised some measure faith, tasted hope, have loved and been loved in an incomplete or limited manner. But these three great pillars in the lives of believers have only been hints, mock-ups of their perfected versions to come. The Infinite Love that awaits followers of Christ will then be truly and completely "known"—and they will finally learn what it is to be fully known and loved.

In the end what awaits you is relationship; perfect relationship. A relationship that no longer has our brokenness standing in the way of true closeness, acceptance, and love, but an unfettered relationship with an infinitely loving God and a restored relationship with His creation.[26]

---

[26] Philippians 3:21 "He will take our weak mortal bodies and change them into glorious bodies like his own, using the same power with which he will bring everything under his control."

GOING
DEEPER

BREAKING GROUND

Has there ever been a time in your life that was "Heaven on earth?"

What about this time made it like Heaven?

Who were you with that made this time so special?

THE DIG

Do you agree or disagree with A.W. Tozer's following statement? "I can safely say, on the authority of all that is revealed in the Word of God, that any man or woman on this earth who is bored and turned off by worship is not ready for Heaven."

Why do you agree or disagree with Tozer's statement?

What does this statement communicate about the reality of heaven?

Read Colossians 1:15-20.
According to scripture, who is Jesus?

What has he done?

Read Revelation 3:20.
What does this statement tell you about the nature of Heaven?

John Piper asks a critical question for every generation, "If you could have heaven, with no sickness, and with all the friends you ever had on earth, and all the food you ever liked, and all the leisure activities you ever enjoyed, and all the natural beauties you ever saw, all the physical pleasure you ever tasted, and no human conflict or any natural disasters, could you be satisfied with heaven, if Christ were not there?"

How do you respond when asked, "Is Jesus the only way to heaven?"

What do you think of Mark's answer to this question? (p. 100)

Read Revelation 21:22
Why is there no need for a temple in heaven?

What is your view of heaven?

In the book, we spoke about the difference between the Destination Gospel and the Relational Gospel. How does one's understanding of the Good News (relational vs. destination) impact how Christians approach presenting the Gospel?

GETTING OUT OF THE HOLE
Watch the Six Symbols of the Gospel presentation found at www.markmcnees.com

SUPPORTING RESOURCES
Here are a few suggestions for continued study:

Wright, N.T. *Surprised by Hope*. New York, NY: HarperCollins, 2009.

McKnight, Scot. *The King Jesus Gospel: The Original Good News Revisited*. Grand Rapids, MI: Zondervan, 2011.

CONCLUSION

CONCLUSION

John and I hope that reading this book has been a fruitful journey, helping you better understand the story of God and His love story with His creation. It is our prayer that through these symbols you will be better equipped to appreciate and convey the whole story of the Good News of Jesus Christ and how you, your friends, and family are the focus of an Infinite Love.

In this final chapter, I wanted to share with you an adapted outline of the Gospel I originally saw in Scott McKnight's book, *The King Jesus Gospel* and offer a Gospel presentation alternative that includes the whole Gospel with God the Father, God the Son, and God the Holy Spirit.

In McKnight's book, he does a great job outlining Paul's presentation of the Gospel in 1 Corinthians 15, but for our purposes, I am going to abbreviate his brilliant exposition to a ready to travel, concise, and understandable whole Gospel outline and presentation.

In this passage, Paul breaks down the Gospel into three parts: Part A is the introduction, part B defines the Gospel, and part C continues Paul's Gospel proclamation. Paul's Gospel statement in 1 Corinthians 15 gives the framework for the whole story of God from creation to second coming.

Part A: Introduction

In the first two verses, Paul is reminding the Corinthians of the Good News he preached and as a result of them "welcoming" and "standing firm" in the Good News, they are saved from eternal separation from their Creator. But, according to Paul, what is the Good News?[27]

Part B: Definition

According to Paul, the Gospel he received and passed on--is not the Four Spiritual Laws, but the Story of Jesus as the fulfillment of the Story of Israel. In other words "Salvation" is not the Gospel, but salvation is actually the result of "welcoming and standing firm" in the Gospel. Here in a remarkably condensed form, Paul establishes five of the six elements of the Gospel: 1) "as the Scriptures said" (Story of Israel), 2) Christ lived, 3) Christ died, 4) He was raised, and 5) He commissioned the church.[28]

Part C: Proclamation of the Continuing Gospel Narrative

In verses 21 and 22, Paul reminds his readers of the original proclamation of the Gospel to Adam and Eve at the point of their betrayal and rebellion against God. In this way, he again stresses the importance of understanding the Story of Israel as revealed in Scripture.[29]

In verses 23-26, he continues the Gospel narrative, directing his attention to the ecclesiastical era (New Testament Church); the era in which we the Church still reside. This is an era characterized by Christians' anticipation of Christ's ultimate return and victory ushering the full reality of Infinite Love. The

---

[27] "Let me now remind you, dear brothers and sisters, of the Good News I preached to you before. You welcomed it then, and you still stand firm in it. It is this Good News that saves you if you continue to believe the message I told you—unless, of course, you believed something that was never true in the first place." (1 Cor 15:1-2, NLT)

[28] "I passed on to you what was most important and what had also been passed on to me. Christ died for our sins, just as the Scriptures said. He was buried, and he was raised from the dead on the third day, just as the Scriptures said. He was seen by Peter and then by the Twelve." (1 Cor 15:3–5, NLT)

[29] "So you see, just as death came into the world through a man now the resurrection from the dead has begun through another man. Just as everyone dies because we all belong to Adam, everyone who belongs to Christ will be given new life." (1 Cor 15:21–22, NLT)

Church and Christ's return completes Paul's proclamation of the Gospel or Good News. In one short chapter, Paul was able to do what took John and me a whole book to do; encapsulate the six major symbols of the Gospel.[30]

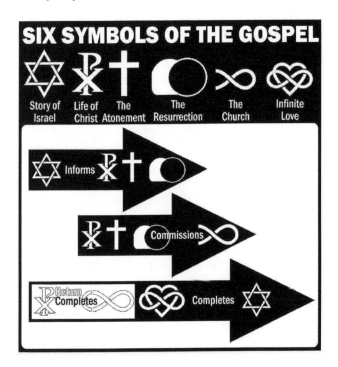

The Story of Israel (The Old Testament) gives understanding of the Life of Christ, Death, and Resurrection. Jesus' resurrection validates His life and death, and commissions the Church. Finally, it is his ultimate return that completes the church, restores Infinite Love (God/Heaven), and completes the Story of Israel.

---

[30] "But there is an order to this resurrection: Christ was raised as the first of the harvest; then all who belong to Christ will be raised when he comes back. After that the end will come, when he will turn the Kingdom over to God the Father, having destroyed every ruler and authority and power. For Christ must reign until he humbles all his enemies beneath his feet. And the last enemy to be destroyed is death." (1 Cor 15:23-26, NLT)

As stated earlier, 1 Corinthians 15 only gives us the framework of the whole Gospel, but I feel it is a great way to solidify the discussion from the earlier chapters. Now with a concise outline of the Gospel, I would like to offer an alternative Gospel presentation.

A New Gospel Presentation

Over the next ten pages I would like to share with you the beginnings of a discipleship journey, through symbols, you can go on with your friends and family.

IDEAL STATE

Unlike what we know today, God's original vision for creation was perfect relational harmony between man, woman, creation, and Himself (Father, Son, and Holy Spirit).[31]

---

[31] Genesis 1:26 Then God said, "Let us make human beings in our image, to be like us. They will reign over the fish in the sea, the birds in the sky, the livestock, all the wild animals on the earth, and the small animals that scurry along the ground."
Genesis 3:8 When the cool evening breezes were blowing, the man and his wife heard the Lord God walking about in the garden. So they hid from the Lord God among the trees.
John 1:1 In the beginning the Word already existed. The Word was with God, and the Word was God.

CURSE: STATE OF HOSTILITY AND ISOLATION

But because of our own selfish ambition to be God instead of in perfect community with God, the curse of isolation and hostility ensued.[32]

Blessing within the Curse

But because God is love, He promised in the midst of the curse that He would make a way back to the Ideal State of perfect harmony between Him and His creation.[33]

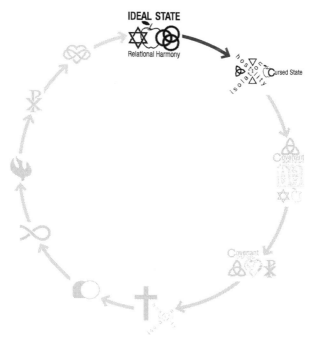

IDEAL STATE

Relational Harmony

Cursed State

---

[32] Genesis 3:16–19 (NLT) Then he said to the woman, "I will sharpen the pain of your pregnancy, and in pain you will give birth. And you will desire to control your husband, but he will rule over you.*" And to the man he said, "Since you listened to your wife and ate from the tree whose fruit I commanded you not to eat, the ground is cursed because of you. All your life you will struggle to scratch a living from it. It will grow thorns and thistles for you, though you will eat of its grains. By the sweat of your brow will you have food to eat until you return to the ground from which you were made. For you were made from dust, and to dust you will return."

[33] Genesis 3:14-15 Then the Lord God said to the serpent, "Because you have done this, you are cursed more than all animals, domestic and wild. You will crawl on your belly, groveling in the dust as long as you live. And I will cause hostility between you and the woman, and between your offspring and her offspring. He will strike your head, and you will strike his heel."

STATE OF LAW

After thousands of years of humanity experiencing hostility and isolation, humanity started to seek out God. But they were not ready for the reestablishment of the Ideal State, so God gave the Law to further show humanity's need for His Grace.[34]

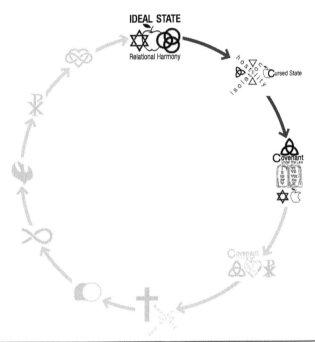

[34] Exodus 20:2–17 (NLT) "I am the Lord your God, who rescued you from the land of Egypt, the place of your slavery. "You must not have any other god but me. "You must not make for yourself an idol of any kind or an image of anything in the heavens or on the earth or in the sea. You must not bow down to them or worship them, for I, the Lord your God, am a jealous God who will not tolerate your affection for any other gods. I lay the sins of the parents upon their children; the entire family is affected—even children in the third and fourth generations of those who reject me. But I lavish unfailing love for a thousand genera- tions on those* who love me and obey my commands. "You must not misuse the name of the Lord your God. The Lord will not let you go unpunished if you misuse his name. "Remember to observe the Sabbath day by keeping it holy. You have six days each week for your ordinary work, but the seventh day is a Sabbath day of rest dedicated to the Lord your God. On that day no one in your household may do any work. This includes you, your sons and daughters, your male and female servants, your livestock, and any foreigners living among you. For in six days the Lord made the heavens, the earth, the sea, and everything in them; but on the seventh day he rested. That is why the Lord blessed the Sabbath day and set it apart as holy. "Honor your father and mother. Then you will live a long, full life in the land the Lord your God is giving you. "You must not murder. "You must not commit adultery. "You must not steal. "You must not testify falsely against your neighbor. "You must not covet your neighbor's house. You must not covet your neighbor's wife, male or female servant, ox or donkey, or anything else that belongs to your neighbor." Romans 7:10b–13 So I discovered that the law's commands, which were supposed to bring life, brought spiritual death instead. Sin took advantage of those commands and deceived me; it used the commands to kill me. But still, the law itself is holy, and its commands are holy and right and good. But how can that be? Did the law, which is good, cause my death? Of course not! Sin used what was good to bring about my condemnation to death. So we can see how terrible sin really is. It uses God's good commands for its own evil purposes.

STATE OF GRACE

After humanity had exhausted itself trying to be good enough to get to God, God, because of His love, came to humanity in the person of Jesus Christ to be love incarnate.[35]

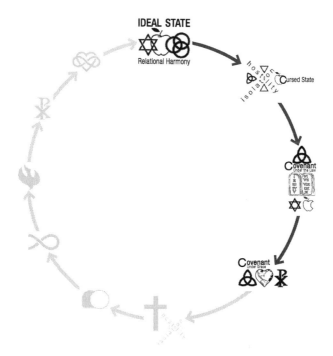

IDEAL STATE

Relational Harmony

Cursed State

Covenant
Under the Law

Covenant
Under Grace

---

35 John 3:16 "For God loved the world so much that he gave his one and only Son, so that everyone who believes in him will not perish but have eternal life.
Romans 5:12–21 When Adam sinned, sin entered the world. Adam's sin brought death, so death spread to everyone, for everyone sinned. Yes, people sinned even before the law was given. But it was not counted as sin because there was not yet any law to break. Still, everyone died—from the time of Adam to the time of Moses—even those who did not disobey an explicit commandment of God, as Adam did. Now Adam is a symbol, a representation of Christ, who was yet to come. But there is a great difference between Adam's sin and God's gracious gift. For the sin of this one man, Adam, brought death to many. But even greater is God's wonderful grace and his gift of forgiveness to many through this other man, Jesus Christ. And the result of God's gracious gift is very different from the result of that one man's sin. For Adam's sin led to condemnation, but God's free gift leads to our being made right with God, even though we are guilty of many sins. For the sin of this one man, Adam, caused death to rule over many. But even greater is God's wonderful grace and his gift of righteousness, for all who receive it will live in triumph over sin and death through this one man, Jesus Christ. Yes, Adam's one sin brings condemnation for everyone, but Christ's one act of righteousness brings a right relationship with God and new life for everyone. Because one person disobeyed God, many became sinners. But because one other person obeyed God, many will be made righteous. God's law was given so that all people could see how sinful they were. But as people sinned more and more, God's wonderful grace became more abundant. So just as sin ruled over all people and brought them to death, now God's wonderful grace rules instead, giving us right standing with God and resulting in eternal life through Jesus Christ our Lord.
Romans 6:14 (NLT) Sin is no longer your master, for you no longer live under the requirements of the law. Instead, you live under the freedom of God's grace.

STATE OF ATONEMENT

Even though God came to offer us grace and to show us how to live, the price of rebellion had to be paid and that "I" which is "SIN" was paid on the cross by Jesus who paid for our selfish ambition and rebellion.[36]

---

[36] Galatians 3:13 (NLT) But Christ has rescued us from the curse pronounced by the law. When he was hung on the cross, he took upon himself the curse for our wrongdoing. For it is written in the Scriptures, "Cursed is everyone who is hung on a tree."*

STATE OF COMMISSION

Three days later Jesus conquered death, rose again, and commissioned His church to be the full expression of God's love in the world.[37]

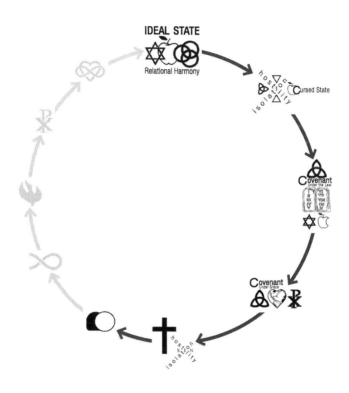

[37] Acts 2:30–31 But he was a prophet, and he knew God had promised with an oath that one of David's own descendants would sit on his throne. David was looking into the future and speaking of the Messiah's resurrection. He was saying that God would not leave him among the dead or allow his body to rot in the grave.
1 Corinthians 15:23 But there is an order to this resurrection: Christ was raised as the first of the harvest; then all who belong to Christ will be raised when he comes back.

STATE OF MISSION

The mission of the body of Christ, the Church, is to make, mature, and mobilize fully devoted followers of Jesus who carry on His instruction to us on how to have a right relationship with God, people, and creation to every nation, tribe, and language.[38]

---

[38] Matthew 28:19–20 Therefore, go and make disciples of all the nations,* baptizing them in the name of the Father and the Son and the Holy Spirit. Teach these new disciples to obey all the commands I have given you. And be sure of this: I am with you always, even to the end of the age."

STATE OF EMPOWERMENT

But we do not do it in our own power, because Jesus sent the Holy Spirit, the same Spirit that raised Him from the dead to indwell in us to carry out the mission of the church.[39]

---

[39] John 14:26 (NLT) But when the Father sends the Advocate as my representative—that is, the Holy Spirit—he will teach you everything and will remind you of everything I have told you.
Romans 8:9–11 But you are not controlled by your sinful nature. You are controlled by the Spirit if you have the Spirit of God living in you. (And remember that those who do not have the Spirit of Christ living in them do not belong to him at all.) And Christ lives within you, so even though your body will die because of sin, the Spirit gives you life* because you have been made right with God. The Spirit of God, who raised Jesus from the dead, lives in you. And just as God raised Christ Jesus from the dead, he will give life to your mortal bodies by this same Spirit living within you.

STATE OF REUNION

Once followers of Christ empowered by the Holy Spirit fulfill the mission to be the full expression of God's love to the whole world, Jesus will come again to usher in the Ideal State 2.0; Infinite Love.[40]

---

[40] John 14:1–3 "Don't let your hearts be troubled. Trust in God, and trust also in me. 2 There is more than enough room in my Father's home. If this were not so, would I have told you that I am going to prepare a place for you? 3 When everything is ready, I will come and get you, so that you will always be with me where I am.

IDEAL STATE 2.0

The Ideal State 2.0 is eternal where there will be no more tears, hurt, or relational pain.[41]

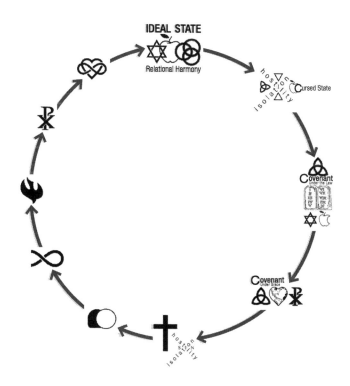

---

[41] Revelation 21:1–4 Then I saw a new heaven and a new earth, for the old heaven and the old earth had disappeared. And the sea was also gone. 2 And I saw the holy city, the new Jerusalem, coming down from God out of heaven like a bride beautifully dressed for her husband. I heard a loud shout from the throne, saying, "Look, God's home is now among his people! He will live with them, and they will be his people. God himself will be with them. 4 He will wipe every tear from their eyes, and there will be no more death or sorrow or crying or pain. All these things are gone forever."

I hope this book has been helpful in giving you a fuller understanding of the Gospel and the story of God. In the beginning of the book I said that I felt compelled to write this book about presenting the Gospel in a simple and concise way because of several disheartening interactions I had recently. Interactions with people who embrace a limited view of the Gospel that perhaps, at best handicaps their faith to an empty, un-relational transaction, void of depth and richness, or at worst allows them to hold on to an unbiblical view of a destination-based faith.

My heart yearns for Christians to be reoriented to the Gospel in all its wonder and mystery. Although this book was written to only lightly scratch a deep theological itch, I hope it has given you the foundation and desire to really dig in and discover the beauty of the Gospel.

FURTHER READING

It's difficult for any one book to do justice to the story of Christianity. Also, theology can be really confusing at times. Other than the footnoted publications, here are some extra resources that may help:

Dallas Willard, *The Divine Conspiracy* (New York, NY: HarperCollins, 1997).

Scott Mcknight, *The King Jesus Gospel: The Original Good News Revisited* (Grand Rapids, MI: Zondervan, 2011).

Stanley Grenz, *Created for Community* (Wheaton, IL: Victor Books, 1996).

Leonard Sweet and Frank Viola, *Jesus Manifesto: Restoring the Supremacy and Sovereignty of Jesus Christ* (Nashville, TN: Thomas Nelson, 2010).

Phillip Yancey, *Prayer: Does It Make Any Difference?* (Grand Rapids, MI: Zondervan, 2010).

N.T. Wright, *Simply Christian: Why Christianity Makes Sense* (New York, NY: HarperOne, 2010).

Eugene Peterson, *A Long Obedience in the Same Direction: Discipleship in an Instant Society* (Downers Grove, IL: InterVarsity Press, 2000).

Richard Hays, *Echoes of Scripture in the Letters of Paul* (New Haven, CT: Yale Univ. Press, 1989); The Conversion of Imagination: Paul as Interpreter of Israel's Scriptures (Grand Rapids: Eerdmans, 2005).

GOING
DEEPER

BREAKING GROUND

What is something you have been "sold" that did not live up to the sales pitch?

THE DIG
Read Matthew 28:18-20

Are you a convert to the religion of Christianity or are you a disciple of Jesus Christ?

What is the difference?

What are some examples of people making converts?

What are some examples of people making disciples?

Read Genesis 1:26, 2:16-23, 3:8, and Revelation 3:20 and 21:1-4

What do these scripture tell us about God's vision for His relationship with His creation?

How does God's relational desire to be with us, differ from the sales pitch of a destination?

Read Genesis 3:1-5, 14-19

What was the original temptation?

What was the relational rift that happened because of the man and woman acting on the temptation of "I."

Read Romans 5:20 and Galatians 3:19

Why was The Law given? What was it's purpose?

Read John 3:16-17

Why did Jesus come?

Read Galatians 3:13

What happened on the cross?

Read 1 Corinthians 15:12-19

Why is the resurrection essential to the Christian faith?

Read Matthew 28:18-20

What is the mission of the church?

Read John 14:26 and Romans 8:9-11

What role does the Holy Spirit have in a believer's life?

Read John 14:1-3

What is Jesus' promise to his Disciples?

Why is this promise the source of our hope?

Read Revelation 21:1-4

What is the central theme of the Gospel?

GETTING OUT OF THE HOLE

Jesus has called us to make disciples, baptize them, and teach them how to follow Christ. Participate in activity that makes disciples of Jesus, not converts. Although making converts is quantifiable, it is not the mission Jesus gave the church. The mission Jesus gave the church is to invite people into a journey toward having a right relationship with God, people, and creation.

APPENDIX I

Symbol One: The Star of David

Hebrews 11:39-40 "All these people earned a good reputation because of their faith, yet none of them received all that God had promised. For God had something better in mind for us, so that they would not reach perfection without us."

Luke 1:30-33 "'Don't be afraid, Mary,' the angel told her, 'for you have found favor with God! You will conceive and give birth to a son, and you will name him Jesus. He will be very great and will be called the Son of the Most High. The Lord God will give him the throne of his ancestor David. And he will reign over Israel forever; his Kingdom will never end!'"

Genesis 1:26-28 "Then God said, 'Let us make human beings in our image, to be like us. They will reign over the fish in the sea, the birds in the sky, the livestock, all the wild animals on the earth, and the small animals that scurry along the ground.' So God created human beings in his own image. In the image of God he created them; male and female he created them. Then God blessed them."

Genesis 2:20-25 "He gave names to all the livestock, all the birds of the sky, and all the wild animals. But still there was no helper just right for him. So the LORD God caused the man to fall into a deep sleep. While the man slept, the LORD God took out one of the man's ribs and closed up the opening. Then the LORD God made a woman from the rib, and he brought her to the man. 'At last!' the man exclaimed, 'This one is bone from my bone and flesh from my flesh! She will be called 'woman,' because she was taken from 'man.'"

Genesis 3:5 "God knows that your eyes will be opened as soon as you eat it, and you will be like God, knowing both good and evil."

Colossians 1:21 "This includes you who were once far away from God. You were his enemies, separated from him by your evil thoughts and actions."

Genesis 3:15b "He will strike your head, and you will strike his heel."

Genesis 3:16 "Then he said to the woman, 'I will sharpen the pain of your pregnancy, and in pain you will give birth. And you will desire to control your husband, but he will rule over you.'"

Genesis 3:17b "…the ground is cursed because of you. All your life you will struggle to scratch a living from it."

Isaiah 7:14 "Look! The virgin will conceive a child! She will give birth to a son and will call him Immanuel (which means 'God is with us')"

Symbol Two: XP

Matthew 5:17 "Don't misunderstand why I have come. I did not come to abolish the law of Moses or the writings of the prophets. No, I came to accomplish their purpose."

Mark 10:45 "For even the Son of Man came not to be served but to serve others and to give his life as a ransom for many."

Colossians 1:16-17 "For through him God created everything in the heavenly realms and on earth. He made the things we can see and the things we can't see—such as thrones, kingdoms, rulers, and authorities in the unseen world. Everything was created through him and for him. He existed before anything else, and he holds all creation together."

John 12:27 "Now my soul is deeply troubled. Should I pray, 'Father, save me from this hour'? But this is the very reason I came!"

John 12:46 "I have come as a light to shine in this dark world, so that all who put their trust in me will no longer remain in the dark."

Matthew 9:11b-13 "Why does your teacher eat with such scum?" When Jesus heard this, he said, "Healthy people don't need a doctor—sick people do." Then he added, "Now go and learn the meaning of this Scripture: 'I want you to show mercy, not offer sacrifices.' For I have come to call not those who think they are righteous, but those who know they are sinners."

Mark 1:38 "We must go on to other towns as well, and I will preach to them, too. That is why I came."

Matthew 10:34 "Don't imagine that I came to bring peace to the earth! I came not to bring peace, but a sword."

Symbol Three: The Cross

Genesis 2:18 "It is not good for the man to be alone. I will make a helper who is just right for him."

Exodus 26:34 "Then put the Ark's cover—the place of atonement—on top of the Ark of the Covenant inside the Most Holy Place."

1 Peter 1:2 "God the Father knew you and chose you long ago, and his Spirit has made you holy."

Symbol Four: The Empty Tomb
1 Corinthians 15:17 "And if Christ has not been raised, then your faith is useless and you are still guilty of your sins."

Colossians 3:3 "For you died to this life, and your real life is hidden with Christ in God"

John 12:23–26 "I tell you the truth, unless a kernel of wheat is planted in the soil and dies, it remains alone. But its death will produce many new kernels—a plentiful harvest of new lives. Those who love their life in this world will lose it. Those who care nothing for their life in this world will keep it for eternity. Anyone who wants to be my disciple must follow me, because my servants must be where I am. And the Father will honor anyone who serves me."

Matt 7:13-14 "The highway to hell is broad, and its gate is wide for the many who choose that way. But the gateway to life is very narrow and the road is difficult, and only a few ever find it."

Exodus 34:14 "You must worship no other gods, for the Lord, whose very name is Jealous, is a God who is jealous about his relationship with you"

Matt 15:7-9 "You hypocrites! Isaiah was right when he prophesied about you, for he wrote, 'These people honor me with their lips, but their hearts are far from me. Their worship is a farce, for they teach man-made ideas as commands from God.'"

Symbol Five: The Fish

Matthew 4:19 "Follow me, and I will make you fishers of men."

Matthew 28:18–20 "I have been given all authority in heaven and on earth. Therefore, go and make disciples of all the nations, baptizing them in the name of the Father and the Son and the Holy Spirit. Teach these new disciples to obey all the commands I have given you. And be sure of this: I am with you always, even to the end of the age."

Luke 9:23 "If any of you wants to be my follower, you must turn from your selfish ways, take up your cross daily, and follow me."

Hebrews 10:25 "And let us not neglect our meeting together, as some people do, but encourage one another, especially now that the day of his return is drawing near."

Luke 14:16b-17 "A man prepared a great feast and sent out many invitations. When the banquet was ready, he sent his servant to tell the guests, 'Come, the banquet is ready.'"

Luke 14:18-20 "But they all began making excuses. One said, 'I have just bought a field and must inspect it. Please excuse me.' Another said, 'I have just bought five pairs of oxen, and I want to try them out. Please excuse me.' Another said, 'I now have a wife, so I can't come.'"

Luke 14:21-24 "The servant returned and told his master what they had said. His master was furious and said, 'Go quickly into the streets and alleys of the town and invite the poor, the crippled, the blind, and the lame.' After the servant had done this, he reported, 'There is still room for more.' So his master said, 'Go out into the country lanes and behind the hedges and urge anyone you find to come, so that the house will be full. For none of those I first invited will get even the smallest taste of my banquet.'"

2 Cor. 5:18-20 "And all of this is a gift from God, who brought us back to himself through Christ. And God has given us this task of reconciling people to him. For God was in Christ, reconciling the world to himself, no longer counting people's sins against them. And he gave us this wonderful message of reconciliation. So we are Christ's ambassadors; God is making his appeal through us. We speak for Christ when we plead, 'Come back to God!'"

John 15:9–11 "Remain in my love. When you obey my commandments, you remain in my love, just as I obey my Father's commandments and remain in his love. I have told you these things so that you will be filled with my joy. Yes, your joy will overflow!"

John 14:12 "I tell you the truth, anyone who believes in me will do the same works I have done, and even greater works, because I am going to be with the Father."

Symbol Six: Infinite Love

Revelation 3:20 "Look! I stand at the door and knock. If you hear my voice and open the door, I will come in, and we will share a meal together as friends"

Colossians 2:17 "For these rules are only shadows of the reality yet to come. And Christ himself is that reality."

Hebrews 10:19 "And so, dear brothers and sisters, we can boldly enter heaven's Most Holy Place because of the blood of Jesus."

Hebrews 10:19 "And so, dear brothers and sisters, we can boldly enter heaven's Most Holy Place because of the blood of Jesus."

Romans 8:15 "So you have not received a spirit that makes you fearful slaves. Instead, you received God's Spirit when he adopted you as his own children. Now we call him, 'Abba, Father'"

Genesis 3:8a "When the cool evening breezes were blowing, the man and his wife heard the LORD God walking about in the garden."

Philippians 3:14 "I press on to reach the end of the race and receive the heavenly prize for which God, through Christ Jesus, is calling us."

Philippians 3:13 "No, dear brothers and sisters, I have not achieved it, but I focus on this one thing: Forgetting the past and looking forward to what lies ahead, I press on to reach the end of the race and receive the heavenly prize for which God, through Christ Jesus, is calling us."

Philippians 3:20 "But we are citizens of heaven, where the Lord Jesus Christ lives. And we are eagerly waiting for him to return as our Savior."

Romans 8:23 "And we believers also groan, even though we have the Holy Spirit within us as a foretaste of future glory, for we long for our bodies to be released from sin and suffering. We, too, wait with eager hope for the day when God will give us our full rights as his adopted children, including the new bodies he has promised us."

James 4:17 "Remember, it is sin to know what you ought to do and then not do it"

Revelation 21:22 "I saw no temple in the city, for the Lord God Almighty and the Lamb are its temple."

1 Peter 1:3–5 "All praise to God, the Father of our Lord Jesus Christ. It is by his great mercy that we have been born again, because God raised Jesus Christ from the dead. Now we live with great expectation, and we have a priceless inheritance—an inheritance that is kept in heaven for you, pure and undefiled, beyond the reach of change and decay. And through your faith, God is protecting you by his power until you receive this salvation, which is ready to be revealed on the last day for all to see."

1 Corinthians 13:12–13 "Now we see things imperfectly, like puzzling reflections in a mirror, but then we will see everything with perfect clarity. All that I know now is partial and incomplete, but then I will know everything completely, just as God now knows me completely. Three things will last forever—faith, hope, and love—and the greatest of these is love."

Conclusion

1 Corinthians 15:1-2 "Let me now remind you, dear brothers and sisters, of the Good News I preached to you before. You welcomed it then, and you still stand firm in it. It is this Good News that saves you if you continue to believe the message I told you—unless, of course, you believed something that was never true in the first place."

1 Corinthians 15:3–5 "I passed on to you what was most important and what had also been passed on to me. Christ died for our sins, just as the Scriptures said. He was buried, and he was raised from the dead on the third day, just as the Scriptures said. He was seen by Peter and then by the Twelve."

1 Corinthians 15:21–22 "So you see, just as death came into the world through a man now the resurrection from the dead has begun through another man. Just as everyone dies because we all belong to Adam, everyone who belongs to Christ will be given new life."

1 Corinthians 15:23-26 "But there is an order to this resurrection: Christ was raised as the first of the harvest; then all who belong to Christ will be raised when he comes back. After that the end will come, when he will turn the Kingdom over to God the

Father, having destroyed every ruler and authority and power. For Christ must reign until he humbles all his enemies beneath his feet. And the last enemy to be destroyed is death."

Genesis 1:26 "Then God said, 'Let us make human beings in our image, to be like us. They will reign over the fish in the sea, the birds in the sky, the livestock, all the wild animals on the earth, and the small animals that scurry along the ground.'"

Genesis 3:8 "When the cool evening breezes were blowing, the man and his wife heard the Lord God walking about in the garden. So they hid from the Lord God among the trees."

John 1:1 "In the beginning the Word already existed. The Word was with God, and the Word was God."

Genesis 3:16–19 "Then he said to the woman, 'I will sharpen the pain of your pregnancy, and in pain you will give birth. And you will desire to control your husband, but he will rule over you.' And to the man he said, 'Since you listened to your wife and ate from the tree whose fruit I commanded you not to eat, the ground is cursed because of you. All your life you will struggle to scratch a living from it. It will grow thorns and thistles for you, though you will eat of its grains. By the sweat of your brow will you have food to eat until you return to the ground from which you were made. For you were made from dust, and to dust you will return.'"

Genesis 3:14-15 Then the Lord God said to the serpent, 'Because you have done this, you are cursed more than all animals, domestic and wild. You will crawl on your belly, groveling in the dust as long as you live. And I will cause hostility between you and the woman, and between your offspring and her offspring. He will strike your head, and you will strike his heel."

Exodus 20:2–17 "I am the Lord your God, who rescued you from the land of Egypt, the place of your slavery. You must not have any other god but me. You must not make for yourself an idol of any kind or an image of anything in the heavens or on the earth or in the sea. You must not bow down to them or worship them, for I, the Lord your God, am a jealous God who will not tolerate your affection for any other gods. I lay the sins of the parents upon their children; the entire family is affected—even children in the third and fourth generations of those who reject me. But I lavish unfailing love for a thousand generations on those who love me and obey my commands. You must not misuse the name of the Lord your God. The Lord will not let you go unpunished if you misuse his name. Remember to observe the Sabbath day by keeping it holy. You have six days each week for your ordinary work, but the seventh day is a Sabbath day of rest dedicated to the Lord your God. On that day no one in your household may do any work. This includes you, your sons and daughters, your male and female servants, your livestock, and any foreigners living among you. For in six days the Lord made the heavens, the earth, the sea, and everything in them; but on the seventh day he rested. That is why the Lord blessed the Sabbath day and set it apart as holy. Honor your father and mother. Then you will live a long, full life in the land the Lord your God is giving you. You must not murder. You must not commit adultery. You must not steal. You must not testify falsely against your neighbor. You must not covet your neighbor's house. You must not covet your neighbor's wife, male or female servant, ox or donkey, or anything else that belongs to your neighbor."

Romans 7:10b–13 "So I discovered that the law's commands, which were supposed to bring life, brought spiritual death instead. Sin took advantage of those commands and deceived me; it used the commands to kill me. But still, the law itself is holy, and its commands are holy and right and good. But how can that be? Did the law, which is good, cause my death? Of course not! Sin used what was good to bring about my condemnation to death. So we can see how terrible sin really is. It uses God's good commands for its own evil purposes."

John 3:16 "For God loved the world so much that he gave his one and only Son, so that everyone who believes in him will not perish but have eternal life."

Romans 5:12–21 "When Adam sinned, sin entered the world. Adam's sin brought death, so death spread to everyone, for everyone sinned. Yes, people sinned even before the law was given. But it was not counted as sin because there was not yet any law to break. Still, everyone died—from the time of Adam to the time of Moses—even those who did not disobey an explicit commandment of God, as Adam did. Now Adam is a symbol, a representation of Christ, who was yet to come. But there is a great difference between Adam's sin and God's gracious gift. For the sin of this one man, Adam, brought death to many. But even greater is God's wonderful grace and his gift of forgiveness to many through this other man, Jesus Christ. And the result of God's gracious gift is very different from the result of that one man's sin. For Adam's sin led to condemnation, but God's free gift leads to our being made right with God, even though we are guilty of many sins. For the sin of this one man, Adam, caused death to rule over many. But even greater is God's wonderful grace and his gift of righteousness, for all who receive it will live in triumph over sin and death through this one man, Jesus Christ. Yes, Adam's one sin brings condemnation for everyone, but Christ's one act of righteousness brings a right relationship with God and new life for everyone. Because one person disobeyed God, many became sinners. But because one other person obeyed God, many will be made righteous. God's law was given so that all people could see how sinful they were. But as people sinned more and more, God's wonderful grace became more abundant. 21 So just as sin ruled over all people and brought them to death, now God's wonderful grace rules instead, giving us right standing with God and resulting in eternal life through Jesus Christ our Lord."

Romans 6:14 "Sin is no longer your master, for you no longer live under the requirements of the law. Instead, you live under the freedom of God's grace."

Galatians 3:13 "But Christ has rescued us from the curse pronounced by the law. When he was hung on the cross, he took upon himself the curse for our wrongdoing. For it is written in the Scriptures, 'Cursed is everyone who is hung on a tree.'"

Acts 2:30–31 "But he was a prophet, and he knew God had promised with an oath that one of David's own descendants would sit on his throne. David was looking into the future and speaking of the Messiah's resurrection. He was saying that God would not leave him among the dead or allow his body to rot in the grave."

1 Corinthians 15:23 "But there is an order to this resurrection: Christ was raised as the first of the harvest; then all who belong to Christ will be raised when he comes back."

Matthew 28:19–20 "Therefore, go and make disciples of all the nations, baptizing them in the name of the Father and the Son and the Holy Spirit. Teach these new disciples to obey all the commands I have given you. And be sure of this: I am with you always, even to the end of the age."

John 14:26 "But when the Father sends the Advocate as my representative—that is, the Holy Spirit—he will teach you everything and will remind you of everything I have told you."

Romans 8:9–11 "But you are not controlled by your sinful nature. You are controlled by the Spirit if you have the Spirit of God living in you. And remember that those who do not have the Spirit of Christ living in them do not belong to him at all. And Christ lives within you, so even though your body will die because of sin, the Spirit gives you life because you have been made right with God. The Spirit of God, who raised Jesus from the dead, lives in you. And just as God raised Christ Jesus from the dead, he will give life to your mortal bodies by this same Spirit living within you."

John 14:1–3 "Don't let your hearts be troubled. Trust in God, and trust also in me. There is more than enough room in my Father's home. If this were not so, would I have told you that I am going to prepare a place for you? When everything is ready,

I will come and get you, so that you will always be with me where I am."

Revelation 21:1–4 "Then I saw a new heaven and a new earth, for the old heaven and the old earth had disappeared. And the sea was also gone. And I saw the holy city, the new Jerusalem, coming down from God out of heaven like a bride beautifully dressed for her husband. I heard a loud shout from the throne, saying, 'Look, God's home is now among his people! He will live with them, and they will be his people. God himself will be with them. He will wipe every tear from their eyes, and there will be no more death or sorrow or crying or pain. All these things are gone forever.'"

APPENDIX II
SUPPORTERS OF THE SIX SYMBOLS OF THE GOSPEL

We would like to thank these and other "unlisted" supporters of the Six Symbols of the Gospel. Through your trust and support we were able to create, produce, and promote the whole Gospel.

Friends

John Meldorf

Jen Ludwig

Douglas Williams

Craig Cooper

Tracy Lee Forrester

Dana Hurst

Valerie Gardner

Teresa Gunter White

Billy Dan Robertson

Pete Butler

Lydia Bickell

Tom L. Fritz

Lori Green

Susan Kemp-Fincham

Amanda Matthews

Paul Hanna

J D Singletary

Michelle McAllister

Nicole Dunaetz

Ben Van Gaasbeek

Lloyd Monroe

Chelle Briggs

Brian Bellamy

John and Rebekah Hagen

Michael and Martha Hanna

Tim and Kelly Sciba

Patron

Heidi Thompson

Russ McNees

Dr. James and Amy Gwartney

Advocate

Susan Coleman

Leroy and Janice McNees

Enthusiast

Tim Singletary

Benefactors

Bubba Meagher

Andrew Paul Bullen

Get Mark's other book:
Immersion: Live the Life God Envisioned for You

A Note from Mark McNees

I would like to invite you to read my first book *Immersion: Live the Life God Envisioned for You*. It can be downloaded via my Facebook page facebook.com/drmarkmcnees2.

It is my prayer that this book will be a blessing and an encouragement to you in your journey as a fellow follower of Christ. I also pray that it will assist you in experiencing the rich and satisfying life Jesus came to give His followers, and that, in the process of reading this book, you will make The Great Commandment the primary grid through which you make all your life decisions.

I have done my best to directly connect the ideas in this book to scriptural passages. Footnotes and textual citations are included on the same page for easy reference and further contextual study.

The book has been organized into seven parts. Part one sets the stage for the five central sections. A seventh and final section is intended as a "putting it all together" framing piece. I have also written a group study which is located at the end of each section with the hope that you will go through this book in community. You can do the studies alone…but everything is better in community.

In the back of the book there is a 40-day life coaching experience, designed to help you experience a richer and more satisfying life.

The greatest blessing to me would be that the body of Christ would be encouraged, equipped, and edified as people join together in their homes for elevated conversations. These group studies are intended to facilitate just such conversations.

In His Grip,
Mark

Connect with Mark
I love people, ideas, stories, and feedback let's keep the conversation going please feel free to connect with me via Facebook (facebook.com/drmarkmcnees2), Twitter (twitter.com/markmcnees), on my blog (markmcnees.blogspot.com), or at markmcnees.com.

Please take the time to post a review of The Six Symbols of the Gospel on Amazon
One of the best ways to promote a book is to review it on Amazon. If you were impacted by The Six Symbols of the Gospel, please take the time to post a review.

Invite Mark to Speak
If your church would like for me to come speak, I would be honored to come. I love meeting new people and sharing God's love.

Invite Mark to Skype
Is your Bible study going through the Going Deepers and would like to discuss the ideas with either John or me? Contact me via Facebook (facebook.com/drmarkmcnees2) and let's set it up.

A FREE PREVIEW OF
Immersion: Live the Life God Envisioned for You

> *"To do anything in this world worth doing, we must not stand back shivering and thinking of the cold and danger, but jump in, and scramble through as well as we can."* -Sydney Smith (1771 - 1845)

I balanced on the edge of the ferry, my hand gripping the rail, my eyes scanning the choppy waters of San Francisco Bay, and thought, Maybe this wasn't such a great idea....

The frigid air made me appreciate my fellow competitors packed in beside me on the ferry; it somehow made what I was about to do seem a little more sane. There was a collective inaudible hum of thoughts processing the looming leap into the inhospitable water. As I watched some choose not to make the leap after all, I too asked myself again if I really wanted to follow through with this increasingly irrational decision. Did I want to do what the California prison system said could not be done? Did I really want to attempt this "Escape from Alcatraz"?

"Escape from Alcatraz" is an annual triathlon held every summer. The race begins with the most daunting task first, the swim from Alcatraz Island to the shores of San Francisco. This uniquely demanding race admits only 2000 athletes from as many as 40 different countries, all converging on San Francisco with one goal in mind: to break out of "The Rock."

The day before the race, I had the opportunity to take a tour of the island. As I walked the halls of the prison and read the stories of those who were incarcerated there, I felt the oppressive air of the concrete and steel, built to keep a relentless grasp on its inhabitants, to choke out all dreams of a better future. Hope and beauty and anticipation of tomorrow were locked out by its 50' barbwire-topped walls and intricate fail-safes, all surrounded by the freezing cold waters of San Francisco Bay.

Swim to Freedom

So, there I was, willingly ferried out to do what wardens and inmates and politicians alike thought was not possible. As we expected – yet still somehow unthinkably – the race officials instructed us one by one to jump into that choppy leviathan several feet below. There was no getting used to the water; it was either, "all in and swim" or "no go and ferry home." Most chose to go, but some chose no.

The moment came: the official pointed at me.

I mustered all my courage and leapt several feet off the ferry – my mind doing its best to prepare my body for the shock of the cold.

When I hit the churning water below I felt my goggles – so crucial to my ability to navigate – rip from my head. Knowing my swim was as good as over without them, I frantically searched for my goggles. On all sides people were jumping in, splashing water in my eyes as they hit, bumping into me as they began their swim.

In the midst of all the commotion, I managed to find my dislodged goggles and pull them back on. At first I was a little disoriented from the chaos of the jump and the goggles and the mass of other swimmers, but soon I found confidence in my preparation. I began to do what I had trained to do, swim to freedom.

Kick, stroke, navigate, breathe, move through the water and get to shore.

The swim was everything I expected and nothing I expected all at once. Yes, there were the tangibles, the cold water, fellow swimmers, and the current. All this I had anticipated intellectually. I knew quite well it was coming. But there was also the reality that I had never experienced anything like this before. I was, at the same time, completely ready and utterly unprepared for the swim ahead.

I had to rely on my focus on my goal of getting to shore. Kick, stroke, navigate, breathe, and move through the water – it was coming together. The familiarity was overriding the unknowns. Until something I had not trained for happened.

From a few yards away, I heard a gurgled shout, "Help!"

At first I thought it was my own subconscious playing tricks on me, a shout from within, from a place that was still unsure of the swim ahead. But then I heard it again, louder this time: "HELP!" As I stopped my stroke, another swimmer drafting behind collided into me. I could feel the current immediately pulling me away from my destination. I struggled with the fact that if I helped there was a good chance my race was over. Surely it was not my responsibility to help someone else. Heck, I was barely making it myself! Finally, squashing the selfishness inside, I swam over toward the call for help.

Scanning the water, I saw an arm flailing in the distance and swam toward it. By the time I reached the now almost catatonic swimmer, a fellow racer arrived on the scene. In unison we called for help, finally getting the attention of the patrol boat. Unfortunately, there were so many swimmers in the water that the driver couldn't navigate his boat safely over to us. A few long minutes later a kayaker with a water gurney came paddling up and was able to tend to the shell-shocked swimmer.

By this time the current had taken me quite some distance from the course, so with effort I struggled to reestablish my path, and began to once again attempt my swim to freedom.

Kick, stroke, navigate, breathe, move through the water and get to shore. The water was rough and the current relentless, but each cycle of my stroke moved me closer to my destination.

At times there was a swarm of swimmers all around me, and other times I felt that I was completely alone. For some reason it seemed easier when I was in a pack of other swimmers, but even that had its challenges. At about the halfway point, when I had finally settled in and was really finding my pace, I was suddenly pulled under water.

Completely submerged, and a bit panicked, thoughts of Jaws ran through my head. What had pulled me under? After a few frantic seconds I discovered the cause of my attack. Another swimmer had grabbed my foot and pulled me under. I am not sure why he did it; maybe he was panicked, maybe he was trying to sabotage my race. Whatever the reason it was so unexpected that it took me several seconds to get back into the rhythm of the race. But, again, my goal and my focus took over: kick, stroke, breathe, move through the water and get to shore.

After 54 minutes I finally reached the shore. A cheering crowd and, more importantly, my friends and family were there to support me in my "escape from Alcatraz."

A Life Immersed

Our faith journey is a lot like swimming from Alcatraz Island. We begin as prisoners to our brokenness faced with a choice. Are we going to serve a life sentence? Or are we going to try to make a break for it – and swim to freedom?

The leap from captivity to freedom can be daunting, even terrifying, as we move from the familiar (as bad as that might be) into the unknown. To be successful it is "all in and swim." There is no getting used to it, there is the ledge and there is the leap – and, waiting for us, the startling water of a complete immersion into faith.

Once we hit the water, unexpected things will happen to us. Perhaps our goggles will be knocked off by the sudden change in environment, as our world view is rocked by our encounter with the one and only living God.

While this is certainly a good thing, it can be scary nonetheless. The world we'd constructed suddenly taken apart and reordered is a frightening prospect, even when the reordering is an infinitely vast improvement. Often we also feel an overwhelming sense of hope flooding into our lives, a beautiful change, but sometimes hard to accept after years of skepticism and disappointment.

Along the way, once we think we are on track we press forward, struggling to stay on the right path, things may arise that make us question whether we truly are on the right track or not. So often these trials of doubt come from unexpected sources, like a fellow swimmer pulling us down as they struggle in their own swim to freedom. Or maybe we have to backtrack or seemingly veer off course to aid another swimmer who is in trouble. Will we find the course again? The doubts stack up quickly.

Through the hindrances and unexpected struggles, again and again we must regain our bearings and resume our swim to freedom. Breathing, navigating, kicking, and pulling for the goal, for ultimately a dry, secure shore awaits – and a host of those who cheer us on.

In the end, being fully immersed in the life God has envisioned for us depends upon the power of God who gives us the ability to finish the race. A life immersed requires that we first leap into the water, learn to breathe in the life giving spirit of God, use our minds to navigate toward the shore, use our strength to kick and pull our strokes, all in concert with each other. This is the redemptive struggle of our swim toward freedom in Christ.

Swimming the Good Race

"I have fought the good fight, I have finished
the race, and I have remained faithful." -Apostle Paul

Jesus was tested by the religious leaders of his day in all kinds of subtle and not so subtle ways. One of these tests came in the form of a simple question. What is the most important commandment? In other words, what is the key to "swimming the good race" according to God? As usual, Jesus' response is both disarmingly simple and profound in its application:

The most important commandment is this: 'You must love the Lord your God with all your heart, all your soul, all your mind, and all your strength.' The second is equally important: 'Love your neighbor as yourself.' No other commandment is greater than these.

Familiarity can be blinding. Psychologists Daniel Simons and Chris Chabris of Harvard University performed a fascinating study demonstrating that humans process very little information once we think we know the situation.

The phenomenon is called "change blindness," when a person only sees what he or she originally took in, blind to the true reality of the situation.

Change blindness is the foundation of magic shows. The audience assumes the most obvious explanation: the hat is a regular hat; the rabbit is the same rabbit the magician just showed them, the pack of cards is a standard set of cards. This is all fine and dandy for magic shows, but when it comes to life, this blindness can have devastating results.

The familiarity of "The Great Commandment" can be a stumbling block. It certainly was with me. The change blindness of what seemed to me like oversaturation in this verse left me thinking I understood it. At some point I stopped processing the depth and significance of Christ's answer to the Pharisees' question.

I have run into similar change blindness in others repeatedly over the past three years while working on my doctorate. When "churched" people asked me what my dissertation or book is about, I used to tell them: living out the Great Commandment in the 21st century. I found that as soon as I mentioned the Great Commandment their demeanor would change. It's become predictable, the sharp shift from interested to dismissive.

Of course, the Great Commandment is not "old news." Christ is the very embodiment of the new. His command is the very core of what our lives are to be about. Jesus' answer to the question from the religious leaders states unequivocally what we are meant to focus on in life in order to achieve the prize. We are to holistically love God and love people.

This book is about answering the question, what would a life look like if a person loved God with all of the heart (emotions), soul (spirit), mind (intellect), strength (physical self), and loved others as themselves (social).

Get the entire book for free! It can be downloaded on my Facebook page facebook.com/drmarkmcnees2.